Do You Like
the Nerdy
Nurse?
Arata
Kawabata

TABLE OF CONTENTS

KAAAN (DAAANG)
KIIIN (DIIING)
KOOON (DOOONG)
Chapter 1:
Spring Anime Are About to Start...
AH.
THERE'S THE SCHOOL NURSE.
MOMOYAMA-SENSEI. ♡

SPRING ANIME ARE ABOUT TO START...

DO I HAVE SPACE ON MY HARD DRIVE?

保健室
GOOD THING IT HAPPENED DURING LUNCH.
SIGN: NURSE'S OFFICE
I'LL HOLD THAT.
HUH? YOU'LL GET BLOOD ON YOU.
IT'S FINE.
TAMOTSU KURITA
I'LL WASH YOUR SHIRT.
SECOND-YEAR MIDDLE SCHOOL STUDENT
ZABU ZABU (SCRUB)
THANKS, KURITA.
ZABU
ZABU

SINCE HIS FIRST YEAR...
...HE'S BEEN A MEMBER OF THE PUBLIC HEALTH COMMIT-TEE.
PAN (FWAP)
ぱん
IT'LL DRY HERE, SO JUST PICK IT UP AFTER SCHOOL.
I'LL BE AROUND.
KURITA...
...YOU'RE ALWAYS IN THE NURSE'S OFFICE.
CAN'T DENY THAT...
YOU CAN ALSO RETURN ...
...THE ICE PACK WHEN YOU STOP BY.
RIGHT!
THANK YOU—!

THIS YEAR, THERE'S A NEW...
...SCHOOL NURSE.
NIJIKO MOMOYAMA.
JIIII (STARE)
じ
STUDENTS AND TEACHERS ALIKE...
...ARE BUZZING ABOUT THE BEAUTIFUL WOMAN WHO'S COME TO THEIR SCHOOL.
DOKI (BADUM)
ドキッ

......
JIII
じー…
M...
MOMOYAMA-SENSEI...?
MM!?
TSUN (POKE)
つん
TSU (WIPE)
YOU HAVE BLOOD ON YOU.
OH... SO I DO.
THERE'S NOT MUCH...
...SO PATTING IT WITH A WET TOWEL SHOULD GET IT OUT.
I GET IT.
WHEN I STAND SO CLOSE...
...TO A BEAUTIFUL WOMAN LIKE THIS...

NU (SLIP)
ぬ
NU
ぬ
NU
ぬ…
POTON (PLOP)
ポトン
SENSEI, SOMETHING FELL.
A MOBILE GAME CHARACTER...
UM, THAT IDOL FROM BAKUMATSU ACADEMY, WHAT WAS IT...?

HWAAAAAH!
IZOU-CHAN!
ZUGYAAAN (KASHOON)
BIKU (TWITCH)
IZOU-CHAN ALMOST ESCAPED ...!

IZ...
IZOU...
IZ...
IZ...
YEAH, THAT'S IT.
IZOU OKADA.
HUH...?
UM...
I-I CAPTURED THIS YESTERDAY...
AH...
I MEAN, UM...

KURITA-KUN...
...YOU'RE ON DUTY DURING LUNCH, AREN'T YOU?
SUN (CALM)
I'M GOING TO GET SOME TEA...
DO YOU WANT SOME?
UH, YES...
UM... SENSEI.
BIKU (TWITCH)
THAT DOLL... IT'S A PRIZE FROM THE ANIMATE LOTTERY, ISN'T IT?
I'VE HEARD THAT'S A TOUGH ONE TO WIN.
......
UZU (SQUIRM)
... WELL...
IT'S A WAR.

E... ESPE-CIALLY WITH ...
...THE PRIZES THIS TIME AROUND!
THIS LOTTERY IS TO COMMEMORATE THE TV ANIME VERSION OF *ISHIN☆LIVE*...
...BUT THE MASCOTS EVERYONE LOVES ARE LEVEL C PRIZES!
S FIGURE ONE TYPE
A
B BATH TOWELS TWO TYPES
C MASCOTS SIX TYPES
D RUBBER PHONE STRAPS TEN TYPES
SO THERE'S A MAD SCRAMBLE FOR LEVEL C — EVEN MORE THAN S AND A!
IN THE PHOTOS ...
...IT DOESN'T REALLY COME ACROSS...
...BUT WHEN I GOT ONE, IT WAS CUTER THAN I IMAGINED!
PAIN-FULLY CUTE!!

COL-LECTING MERCH...
...IS ABOUT INFORMATION WAR-FARE.
WHEN THERE'S A PRIZE I WANT...
...I CHECK WHICH CONVENIENCE STORES HAVE IT.
Lottery Simulat
THEN I RUN A SIMULATION SEVERAL TIMES...
...AND PLAN MY BUDGET.
FOOD, CLOTHING, AND SHELTER...
...ARE AFTER-THOUGHTS.
MOMOYAMA-SENSEI'S SPECIAL LOW-COST LUNCH, HEAVY ON BEAN SPROUTS AND TOFU
TO ME, THESE ARE NECESSARY EXPENSES!
10K
10K
10K
10K
I DON'T WANT TO LET THEM GET AWAY...
...BECAUSE I KNOW...
...THE JOY OF OBTAINING THEM AND THE FRUS-TRATION OF MISSING OUT ON THEM!
WHEN I GET THE CHANCE...
ORIGINAL SCRIPT
AUTO-GRAPH
...I EVEN BUY ORIGINAL KEY FRAMES!
KEY FRAME
FOR THAT...
GU (CLENCH)

...I WOULD EVEN...
...GIVE UP AN ORGAN.
DO (WHUP)
KIIN (DIIING)
KOOON (DOOONG)
KAAAN (DAAANG)
"IN SPRING, THE DAWN...
"... GROWING LIGHT LITTLE BY LITTLE..."
THAT WAS AN INCREDIBLE LUNCH PERIOD...
GROAN...
I WASN'T THINKING AND JUST STARTED TALKING...
WHAT KIND OF SCHOOL NURSE AM I...?

Do You Like the Nerdy Nurse?

Do You Like
the Nerdy
Nurse?

GAYA (GAB)
ガヤ
THE NEW SCHOOL NURSE IS REALLY SOMETHING, ISN'T SHE?
WHAT'S HER NAME, NIJIKO MOMOYAMA?
GAYA
ガヤ
I WANNA BE LIKE HER WHEN I GROW UP.
THAT KINDA COOL WOMAN...
Chapter 2:
The Shipping Is Sublime.
FORGET ABOUT IT. PERSONALITY-WISE, YOU'RE NOTHING LIKE HER...
...AND YOUR LEGS ARE TOO SHORT.
HUH!?
HOW DARE YOU!?
ヒョコ
HYOKO (HOP)
HYOKO
ヒョコ
SIGN: NURSE'S OFFICE
BEEN A WHILE SINCE I'VE HAD A NASTY SCRAPE LIKE THIS...
HYOKO
ヒョコ
HYOKO
ヒョコ
保健室
I WONDER IF MOMO-YAMA-SENSEI IS IN.

MOJI (FIDGET)
もじ
MOJI
もじ
MOJI
もじ
MOJI
もじ
HAA (SIGH)
はあ、
PURU (SHIVER)
プル
THANK YOU...
PURU
プル
PURU
プル
...GOD!
I GUESS IT'S HER LUNCH BREAK TOO.
...I WONDER WHAT SHE'S READING.
PATA (FAN)
パタ
PATA
パタ
READING THE SAME PAGE OVER AND OVER
A LIGHT NOVEL?
EXCUSE ME.
I'M KURITA, A SECOND-YEAR.
GARA (SLIDE)
ガラ

パァン
PAAN (FWAP)
PI (FWISH)
SUKON (FWOOP)
スコン
......
IS SOMETHING WRONG ...?
IS THERE A BREEZE IN HERE...?
SUU (SHFF)
スウッ
...I SKINNED MY KNEE.
I'LL PUT A BANDAGE ON IT.

......
ばっ
BA (TURN)
そわ
SOWA (FIDGET)
そわ
SOWA
......
HUH?
THAT'S WHAT SHE WAS READING.

BIKU (TWITCH)
WHAT KIND OF BOOK WERE YOU READING WHEN I CAME IN?
KASHAAAN (CLATTER)
A N-NOVEL...
R-ROMANCE...
KATA (SHUDDER) KATA KATA KATA
M...
MOMO-YAMA-SENSEI ...?
UM, I...
I LOVE LIGHT NOVELS.
I'M INTO ANIME TOO.
HOW ABOUT GAMES ?
I-I PLAY MOBILE GAMES...
ME TOO!

MM...
PLAY...
PLAY?
PLAYING TOO MANY GAMES...
KIRI (GLEAM)
...ISN'T GOOD.
AND OF COURSE, IT'S BAD TO PAY FOR ITEMS IN MOBILE GAMES.
YOU SHOULD HAVE A VARIETY OF INTERESTS...
YOU SOUND LIKE A TEACHER!
WELL, I AM AN EDUCATOR.
SO...
...MY FAVORITE MOBILE GAME...
...IS FGO.
...!?
FGO...!
SFX: KASHAAAN
THE NEWEST EVENT IS AWESOME!
...YEAH.
THERE'S A WAR AND A REVOLUTION...
YEAH.
...SO IT'S GOT BATTLE ROYALES.
BUT ALSO CHARACTER RELATIONSHIPS ON THE BAD GUYS' SIDE...
......!

SHIPPING: ROMANTIC CHARACTER PAIRINGS (IN ORIGINAL WORKS OR FAN FICTION)

HE'S GOT THAT COMPLEX, SO THE WAY HE TRIES SO HARD IN FRONT OF HER IS JUST, OH!
HIS EXPRESSIONS AND HOW HE CLENCHES HIS FIST...
HE'S GOT A CONTRACT WITH HER...
...BUT WHEN I SAW THAT, TO BE HONEST, I WAS CURIOUS ABOUT HIS REACTION.
I MEAN...
...PERSONALLY, I LOVE THE BATTLE SYSTEM.
YEAH.
YEAH.
IT'S LIKE, THANK YOU, COMMAND SPELL VOICES.
COMMAND SPELL VOICES: LINES HEARD WHEN A MASTER GIVES AN UNDEFIABLE COMMAND IN BATTLE
I CAN'T WAIT TO SEE WHAT HAPPENS NEXT!

I FEEL LIKE I'M BEING SPURRED ON...
AH...
S-SORRY... YOU DON'T WANT TO HEAR THAT...
N-NO, IT'S FINE!
I KNOW WHAT YOU MEAN!
SHE MUST HAVE A GREAT TIME PLAYING IT.
MOMOYAMA-SENSEI...
SURPRISINGLY...
...I'M SOMEWHAT ENVIOUS.
PATA (FAN)
ぱた
PATA
ぱた
PETA (STICK)
ぺた
I WANNA TALK TO HER AGAIN.

Do You Like the Nerdy Nurse?

Do You Like the Nerdy Nurse?

MOMO-CHAN-SENSEI! ♡
DO YOU HAVE A BOY-FRIEND?
I DO NOT.
Chapter 3:
Do You Have Any Openings on Your Friend List?
YEAH, BUT I'M SURE YOU HAVE IN THE PAST.
WHAT DID YOU DO WHEN YOU WERE WITH YOUR BOYFRIEND?
I DON'T ...
... JUST SEE ANY TWO GUYS AND THINK "SHIP AWAY!"...
UGYAAAN (CACKLE)
SENSEI, LOOK!
YUSSA (HUMP)
GISHI (CREAK)
THAT'S NOT...
...THE KIND OF FUJOSHI I AM.
BOYS' LOVE! BOYS' LOVE!
GISHI
YUSSA
P...
PARDON ME. I HAVE AN ERRAND ...

FORGET IT!!!!
FORGET IT, FORGET IT, FORGET IT, FORGET IT, FORGET IT!
WERE MIDDLE SCHOOL BOYS...
...ALWAYS SO VULGAR!?
PURE, CON-FLICTED...
...AND SOMETIMES PASSION-ATE!
IT HAS TO BE THAT KIND OF ROMANCE...!
JUST BECAUSE I'M A HUGE (CLOSETED) BL FAN...
...DOESN'T MEAN I DON'T HAVE STANDARDS!!

DON (BUMP)
S...
SORRY...
KURITA-KUN...
MOMO-YAMA-SENSEI!
HELLO.
A WALKING, TALKING SAFETY ZONE...!!
PEKAAA (FLASH)
SENSEI, WHAT'S WRONG?
IS THERE SOME-THING IN YOUR EYE?
NO, IT'S NOTHING...
HE MAKES ME FEEL SO AT EASE...!

OH, SENSEI ...
DO YOU HAVE ANY OPEN SPOTS ON YOUR *FGO* FRIEND LIST?
HUH...?
LIKE ...
...THE WHOLE FRIEND-SUPPORT THING IS WAY EASIER WHEN YOU ACTUALLY KNOW THE PERSON.
HUH!? WHA...? GOD...!
Y...
YES, I'VE GOT OPEN SPOTS!
GREAT, THEN I'LL SEND A FRIEND REQUEST.
...THEN YOU WOULD CHANGE YOUR SUPPORTS...?
SURE.
JUST DM ME WHEN YOU WANT ME TO CHANGE MY LINEUP.
I-INCREDIBLE... HE REALLY IS...
...A "FRIEND" !!
I'VE NEVER MET...
...ANYONE LIKE YOU!

AH!
MOMOYAMA-SENSEI!
HI, SENSEI!!
SENSEI!!
SENSEI!!
ZUGYAAAN (KASHOOM)
AH!
THAT'S RIGHT...
I'M...
...A "SENSEI."
SCHOOL NURSE
NIJIKO MOMOYA
MITSUGI MIDD
I WAS ONLY RECENTLY SCOLDED...
...FOR HAVING PERSONAL CONVER-SATIONS WITH A STUDENT!
AH! MOMO-YAMA-SENSEI...
...IS ESPE-CIALLY FRIENDLY WITH KURITA-KUN!
YOU MUSTN'T DO THAT, MOMO-YAMA-SENSEI!
BUT...
BUT...
BUT...!
UGH...

BUT IF IT'S A SECRET ACCOUNT ...
...THAT MIGHT JUST WORK...?
PIKYUUUN (FWIIING)
YES, THAT'S IT...!
NO PROBLEM IF I'M JUST ANOTHER FGO PLAYER!
IT'LL BE AN FGO PLAYER CONNECTING WITH ANOTHER FGO PLAYER.
THERE'S NOTHING WRONG WITH THAT!!
YEAH, THAT'S HOW WE'LL DO IT!
THINKS SHE'S ESPECIALLY SHARP TODAY
THINKS SHE'S OVER-THINKING IT
DAYS LATER, SHE CREATED A PRIVATE ACCOUNT AND THEY CONNECTED.

Do You Like the Nerdy Nurse?

Do You Like the Nerdy Nurse?

Chapter 4:
I Warned You About Spending Money on Mobile Games
22:05
@t_momomomo_t
One minute ago
Executed
Pulled for favorite character, flopped
TRANSLATION: SHE PAID MONEY TO RAISE THE ODDS OF WINNING HER FAVORITE CHARACTER IN A MOBILE GAME "LOTTERY" BUT STILL DIDN'T GET HIM.
INU NO OMAWARISAN
M-MOMOYAMA-SENSEI...
MOMOYAMA-SENSEI AND KURITA-KUN, CONNECTED BY A SECRET ACCOUNT
@t_momomomo_t
...YOU HAVE MY DEEPEST SYMPATHIES...!!
MOMOYAMA-SENSEI IS IN HIGH SPIRITS TODAY.
WHEN SHE'S AROUND, IT MAKES EVERYONE CHEERFUL.
MAYBE SHE'S IN A BETTER MOOD THAN I THOUGHT.
Sanitation Month
CLEAN SCHOOL, CLEAN HEART

AH.
MOMO-YAMA-SENSEI.
YOU MAY HAVE ...
ぴと
PITO (FWAP)
...A SLIGHT FEVER.
HUH!?
DO YOU WANT TO...
...LIE DOWN FOR A WHILE?
WHAT'S WITH HER???
SHE'S GRINNING AND BEING ASSERTIVE...
HUH...?
......

保健室
EXCUSE ME...
SIGN: NURSE'S OFFICE
ぐた…
GUTA (SLUMP)
ガッタン
GATTAN (RATTLE)
Y-YES.
YES?
PROB-LEM?
OH... KURITA-KUN.
IS SOME-THING WRONG?
UM, NOT WITH ME...
SENSEI...
...ARE YOU ALL RIGHT?

OH... UM...
ABOUT MY PULLS...?
I...
I WARNED YOU...
...ABOUT SPENDING MONEY ON MOBILE GAMES...
...B-BUT EVEN THOUGH I'M AN ADULT...
...I DIDN'T STICK TO MY BUDGET.
I FAILED.
A-AS AN EDUCATOR ...
...I FAILED!
AND I'M BROKE!
S...
SO...

...I'LL WORK HARD...
...AND RECOVER...
I'LL WORK LONG HOURS...
...AND SAVE MY MONEY...
SENSEI, IF YOU WORK LONGER HOURS...
...DO YOU MAKE MORE MONEY?
NO.
MAYBE I'M NOT CUT OUT TO BE A SCHOOL NURSE...!
WHA—!?
I WOULD...
...HATE TO SEE YOU GO.
AH...
R... REALLY...?

THANK YOU.
I'M GLAD...
HUH?
AH...
...YOU'RE HERE TOO, KURITA-KUN.
UM...
?
DOKI
!?
DOKI (BADUM)
Y-YOU'RE WELCOME!
DA (DASH)

Do You Like the Nerdy Nurse?

Do You Like the Nerdy Nurse?

MOMO-CHAN-SENSEI!
GOOD MORNING.
YOU'RE AS BEAUTIFUL AS EVER, SENSEI.
NIJIKO MOMO-YAMA-SENSEI...
...IS THE NEW...
...SCHOOL NURSE.
Chapter 5:
His Name Is Yuya Kazami...

SHE'S KIND OF DIFFER- ENT...
...FROM ALL THE OTHER GIRLS HERE.
HUH...? KURITA, WHY DO YOU KEEP STARING AT US?
EWWW, WHAT A CREEP!
I-I'M NOT STARING.

KIIN (DIIING)
KOOON (DOOONG)
KAAAN (DAAANG)
THE NURSE'S OFFICE...
I WONDER IF MOMOYAMA-SENSEI IS IN.
CHIRA (GLANCE)
WHY DO YOU KEEP LOOKING AT THE NURSE'S OFFICE?
DO YOU HAVE A CRUSH ON MOMO-CHAN?
HUH? WHAT?
WHAT ARE YOU TALKING ABOUT!?
WHAAA!?
WHY WOULD YOU THINK THAT?
保健室
THE ONLY WAY I'LL KNOW IF SHE'S IN IS BY CHECKING...
OH... SHE'S NOT ALONE...
SIGN: NURSE'S OFFICE

UGU (SOB)
UGU
GU
SUN (CALM)
M-MAYBE A COUPLE'S SPAT...?
WAAAAAAAH!
WHY DOES HE...
...IGNORE ME!?
WHAT DID...
...I DOOO!?
WHAT A PAIN.
SHUT UP.
ZUBIBI (HONK)
BIBI
IF I SAY OR DO SOMETHING HE DOESN'T LIKE, HE JUST IGNORES ME!
WHAT'S WITH HIM!?!?
SKREEEEE!
I... I SEE...
WAAAAAAAAAH!
ULP...
THE NURSE'S OFFICE ISN'T JUST FOR INJURIES AND SICKNESS...
...BUT PEOPLE ALSO COME FOR ADVICE.

GARA (SLIDE)
OH.
I'M NOT REALLY HERE FOR ANYTHING...
Sorry.
Wait here.
O...
OKAY...
WAAAH... THANK YOU.
GARA
GUESS I'LL BE GOING TOO.

TH-THANKS FOR WAITING...
NO PROBLEM.
SEN-SEI...
ARE YOU OKAY...?
RIGHT AFTER GOLDEN WEEK, ESPE-CIALLY...
...A LOT OF STUDENTS WANT AN EXCUSE NOT TO GO BACK TO CLASS.
NOT THAT I BLAME THEM...
TH-THAT GIRL BEFORE...
...SEEMED REALLY UPSET.
THAT'S PART OF IT...
...BUT I'VE ALSO BEEN CAUGHT UP IN THE LAST-MINUTE RUSH FOR THE FGO EVENT...
LACK OF SLEEP.
YEAH, YOU DO HAVE TO GRIND FOR MATERIALS...

I HAVE TO SEPARATE THESE BY CLASS.
DOSA (WHUMP)
ドサッ
PAPERS: HEALTH BULLETIN
I'M NOT IN A CLUB...
...AND HAVE FREE TIME...
...SO I CAN ALWAYS HELP OUT!
YOU SHOULD THINK BEFORE YOU COMMIT...
I AM GRATEFUL, THOUGH.
PERA PERA (FLIP)
ペラ ペラ
KASA (RUSTLE)
カサ
KASA
カサ
UZU (FIDGET)
うず
UZU
うず
CHIRA (GLANCE)
チラ
CHIRA
チラ
BY THE WAY, SENSEI...
...YOU SAW THE NEW CONAN MOVIE, DIDN'T YOU?
HOW WAS IT?
BIKU (TWITCH)
ビクッ
Executed
Pulled

YES, ABOUT THAT...!!
GATAAAN (RATTLE)
ガタ
ン
I...
...HAD ABSOLUTE CONFIDENCE ...
GU (CLENCH)
...THAT I WOULDN'T BECOME AN AMUPI FAN!
GU
GU
GU
BUT...
...THEN ...
...I WAS AMBUSHED.

TUNKU (THUNK)
HIS NAME...
...IS YUYA KAZAMI.
© GOSHO AOYAMA/SHOGAKUKAN
HE'S A STRAITLACED COP WHO'S LIKE A FAITHFUL DOG TO THE NATION AND HIS BOSS, SO YOU ALSO FEEL SORRY FOR HIM. THOSE ELEMENTS ARE AWESOME...
...BUT MORE THAN ANYTHING...
...HIS BOSS IS A YOUNGER, HANDSOME GORILLA!!
MEANING KIND MAN + TOUGHNESS
CHARACTER PAIRINGS ARE IMPORTANT, HUH?
PAPER: HEALTH BULLETIN
SENSEI...
...YOU'VE STOPPED MOVING.
AH! SORRY...
FUNYASHINAAA (DROOPY)
AHHH...
PURU (QUIVER)
MY PALM SWEAT IS DRENCHING THE PAPERS...
PURU
PURU
PURU

GROSS...
A LACK OF SLEEP AND GETTING WORKED UP HAVE PRODUCED WEIRD PERSPIRATION...
BEKO (FAN)
BEKO
SENSEI, TAKE A FEW DEEP BREATHS.
HOOOO... HAAAA...
CALMED DOWN
I JUST...
...HAVE SO MANY THINGS ON MY MIND RIGHT NOW.
I THOUGHT I'D GO ALL IN ON KAZAMI-SAN...
...BUT HE FOLLOWS THE PATTERN.
PERA (FLIP)
ONE AFTER ANOTHER, I COME TO LOVE THESE (TWO-DIMENSIONAL) PEOPLE...
...I HAD NO INTEREST IN BEFORE.

THE DAY...
...I BECOME AN AMUPI FAN...
...MAY NOT BE THAT FAR AWAY AFTER ALL.
YOU'VE GOT A LOT GOING ON IN YOUR HEAD...
TON (TAP)
TON
I SUPPOSE ...
BUT THE STRANGE THING IS...

...I'VE STARTED ...
...THINKING THAT I'D LIKE TO COOK...
...FOR KAZAMI-SAN.
I SURPRISED MYSELF.
I MEAN, NO MATTER HOW YOU SLICE IT...
...I'M SURE AMUPI CAN COOK SOMETHING FIVE HUNDRED TIMES TASTIER.
IN THE FIRST PLACE ...
...THERE'S NOTHING I HAVE TO OFFER HIM.
I GUESS ONLY MONEY...
MOMO-YAMA-SENSEI ...

YOU'RE SEPARATED BY A DIMENSIONAL BARRIER ANYWAY...
...SO THERE'S NO NEED TO COMPETE WITH ANYONE.
YOU'RE FREE TO FEEL WHATEVER YOU WANT...
...ABOUT WHOMEVER YOU WANT.
IT'S BEEN A WHILE SINCE I'VE FALLEN THIS HARD FOR SOMEONE (WHO'S TWO-DIMENSIONAL) ...
...SO I FEEL LIKE I'M WALKING ON AIR.
SIIIGH...
TON (TAP)
I MUST...

...HAVE A WEAKNESS...
ほけんだより

...FOR SAD SACKS (BUT ONLY THE TWO-DIMENSIONAL KIND).

AS SHE THOUGHT ABOUT THE (TWO-DIMENSIONAL) MAN SHE LOVED...
...MOMOYAMA-SENSEI'S FACE IN PROFILE...
...WAS SO BEAUTIFUL.
I WAS DAZZLED.
AH!
I BLABBED WITHOUT THINKING AGAIN...!

Do You Like
the Nerdy
Nurse?

Do You Like the Nerdy Nurse?

GUI (PULL)
ぐい
ZAPU (SPLISH)
ざぷ
ZAPU
ざぷ
Chapter 6:
Kids' Anime Is Medicine for the Soul

URU (SOB)
うる

M...
MOMOYAMA-SENSEI...?
MAYBE SOMETHING HAPPENED?
L-LIFE CAN BE ROUGH FOR ADULTS TOO...
OR RATHER...
...LIFE CAN BE ROUGH BECAUSE YOU'RE AN ADULT.
BUT I DON'T UNDERSTAND.
I DON'T UNDERSTAND ADULTS YET.

KYU
(SQUEAK)
きゅ…
5月月間スケジュール
I WAS TIRED, SO I WENT HOME EARLY.
FRIDAY EVENING.
I RAN-DOMLY...
...PUT ON A SHOW.
AT FIRST...
...I JUST THOUGHT IT WAS CUTE...
...SO I KEPT WATCHING.

JIWA (TRICKLE)
じわ…

IT WAS ANIME FOR KIDS...
...BUT...
...IT WAS VERY SOOTHING.
IN THAT WORLD...
...NOBODY IS OSTRA-CIZED...
...AND NOBODY GETS SNEERED AT.
He can't even do that. Honestly, he's a total loser. I wish he'd just go away and never come back.
I know, sooooo disgusting!
EWW!
NO BOYS ALLOWED!
DON'T BRING A BABY ON THE TRAIN!

THERE ARE CHAL-LENGES ...
...AND FAILURES...
...BUT EVERY-ONE...
...IS CHEERFUL AND UNDER-STANDING.
WHEN THE GOING GETS TOUGH, THEY SMILE.
GYU (SQUEEZE)
ぎゅ

......I BECAME...
...A BIT OF A COWARD.
"I'LL SINK MYSELF INTO THIS OBSESSION."
危険 底なし沼
AS SOON AS I THOUGHT THAT, I WASN'T ABLE TO STEP AWAY.
THERE ARE A LOT OF CUTE KIDS...
...AND VARIOUS RELATIONSHIPS.
SIGN: DANGER, BOTTOMLESS BOG
WHEN THERE ARE MANY CHARACTERS...
...I'LL ALWAYS FIND A FAVORITE.

KIDS' ANIME...
...IS MEDICINE...
...FOR THE SOUL.

KIDS' ANIME...
I USED TO WATCH IT BACK IN ELEMENTARY SCHOOL, BUT DID IT HAVE THAT EFFECT?
SO MUCH THAT RECALLING IT...
...BRINGS TEARS TO HER EYES?

SHE'S BEAUTI-FUL...

AHHH
...
GETTING WORKED UP ABOUT IT BROUGHT TEARS TO MY EYES...
BIKU (TWITCH)
DON'T USE THE DUST RAG!!
H-HANDKER-CHIEF...
!
I USED IT MYSELF AFTER GOING TO THE BATH-ROOM...
YIKES!
I CAN'T GIVE THAT TO HER...!
H-HERE! USE A TISSUE!
SHUBA (FWISH)
THANK YOU.

YET AGAIN YOU SEE ME...
...ACTING SHAME-FULLY.
ULP!
AH HA HA!
BUT I WAS SURPRISED.
AH HA HA!

I'M SURE.
HEH HEH...
SORRY FOR...
...SUR-PRISING YOU, THEN.
EH, IT HAPPENS.
AH HA HA.
HEH.
DO PEOPLE SAY THAT YOU REMIND THEM OF KIDS' ANIME?
ZUZU (SIP)
ズズ
HUH...?

Do You Like the Nerdy Nurse?

Do You Like the Nerdy Nurse?

Chapter 7:
Workplace Escape!!
GAKO (CLUNK)
ガコッ

AND I'M OUTTA THERE!!
ガタン
GATAN (CLANK)
GOTON (CLUNK)
ゴトン
KOTSU
コツ
KOTSU (CLACK)
コツ
KOTSU
コツ

KYAN
KYAN
KYAN
KYAN
KYAN
KYAN
KYAN
KYAN
KYAN
KYAN
WAN
KYAN (ARF)
WAN (BARK)
KYAN
KYAN
KYAN
KYAN
……
OH, SORRY.
KYAN
KYAN
KYAN
NOT AT ALL. THEY'RE SO CUTE.
KYAN
KYAN
KYAN
KYAN
KYAN
WAFU (WOOF)

AHHHH...
HOWA (GLEAM)
KYAN (ARF)
KYAN
KYAN
BAKUMATSU ACADEMY IDOL GAME
ISHIN☆LIVE
KYAN
KYAN
TAKECHI-SAN
DON'T EVEN THINK YOU HAVE A CHANCE...
...AT BEATING US WITH A MIC!
KYAN
IZOU-CHAN
IT WAS LIKE SEEING TAKECHI-SAN AND IZOU-CHAN.

DISCOUNTED SUSHI!
20%引き
にぎり鮨盛10貫
PACKAGING: 20% OFF / SUSHI TEN-PIECE BONANZA
GOOD LUCK LEVEL A...!
JI (STARE)
じ……
チケット
大人:1500円
POSTER: EXHIBIT / TICKETS—ADULT: 1,500 YEN
WHOA!
18:16
TA (DASH)
たっ

LABEL: SHISHINOANA

Watch in real time: success
SORUTO
FROM WHAT I COULD TELL FROM LAST WEEK'S PREVIEW...
...THIS ONE...
...SHOULD BE AN INCREDIBLE EPISODE!

PACKET: SOY SAUCE
MM...
MMM...
HFF ...
HFFF...
WHA...
WHAT'S THAT...?
ZEE (WHEEZE)
ZEE
MY TIME-LINE'S BLOWING UP.
????? Omigod???
Huh? So are they married, then?
Middle-aged couple
Awesome
It's huge that they made it official

TSU (CLICK)
TSU
Ugh, I can't get enough
25分前
They made it official...? (jumping for joy)
25分前
Great animation
12分前
About that???
4分前
is great too.
shows what they were thinking before they acted.
3
TON (TAP)
I KNOW...
Make a movie version already
2
EEK!
Today's you-know-what
A DRAWING OF IT ALREADY!
56
3
I...
I'LL WATCH IT ONCE MORE...

POCHI (CLICK)
ポ4
POCHI
ポ4
AWESOME...
THE ART IS GORGEOUS...
POCHI
ポ4
ポ4
POCHI
※ GOING FRAME BY FRAME

PIRORON (RIIING)
PIRO
SHAN (SHING)
SHAN
SHAN

ティロリロ♪
TIRORIRO (JINGLE)
ティロリロ♪
TIRORIRO
TIRORIRO
Snooze
Stop
6:00
ティロリロ
URK...
I FELL ASLEEP WHILE PLAYING...!

Do You Like
the Nerdy
Nurse?

Do You Like the Nerdy Nurse?

Chapter 8:
Those Who Believe Will Be Saved...!!

IN THE GACHA SIMULATOR, IT TOOK ME AN AVERAGE...
...OF TWO HUNDRED SIXTY STONES.
PAN (CLAP)
ぱんっ
PAN
ぱんっ
I'VE BROUGHT ALL MY STONES TOGETHER...
FANS: TAKECHI / COME HOME
...SO IF I CAN GET THIS WHILE SPENDING LESS THAN TWENTY THOUSAND YEN, IT'LL BE A MAJOR SUCCESS.

10x Scout
PULL...!!
MOMO-YAMA-SENSEI...?
BIKU (JUMP)
K-K-KURITA-KUN!?
WHY ARE YOU OUT THIS LATE!?
I WAS TALKING TO A FRIEND AFTER HIS CLUB MEETING WAS OVER, AND WE LOST TRACK OF TIME.
THEN I SPOTTED YOU ON THE WAY HOME...
KOSO KOSO (SNEAK)
SO... UM...

WHAT IS THAT?
THAT
FANS: TAKECHI-SAN / COME HOME
NOT HIDDEN...
...AT ALL

AH!
WAIT, WAIT, UM...
ISHIN ☆ LIVE'S...
...SCOUT GACHA.
RIGHT? I SAW IT ON MY TIMELINE.
JUNE EVENT
イベントスカウト
SCREEN: EVENT SCOUT / WATER FESTIVAL
YOU WANT TO SCOUT TAKECHI-SAN?
YES...
THE FIVE-STAR RATE'S 1.25% THIS TIME...
TEXT: HANPEITA
PULLING A FIVE-STAR'S ALWAYS TOUGH IN ANY GAME.
I KNOW!
I KNOW!
SO...
...YOU CAME HERE.
AS I RECALL...
YOU KNOW IT?

MITSUGI MIDDLE SCHOOL'S...
...SACRED MATCH-MAKING SITE.
I-IS IT TRUE...?
I JUST HEARD ABOUT IT FROM A GIRL IN CLASS.
I DON'T KNOW...
I'VE ONLY HEARD RUMORS...
I CAN'T AFFORD TO GO OVER BUDGET AGAIN...
......
...SO I'M WILLING TO GIVE ANYTHING A SHOT.
I HAVE NO CHOICE BUT TO DEPEND ON THE POWER OF THE OCCULT...!

YOU WOULD HATE TO REGRET NOT TRYING IT LATER, RIGHT?
KURITA-KUN...
FAN: TAKECHI-SAN
PLEASE...
PLEASE FORM A CONNECTION...
...BETWEEN TAKECHI-SAN AND ME.

IT'LL WORK...! IT HAS TO!!
THOSE WHO BELIEVE WILL BE SAVED...!!
武

WELL...
...HERE I GO!
TO (TAP)
PAA (FLASH)

Y-YOU GOT HIM ...!
WOW!
S-SENSEI.
DON'T YOU WANT TO GET A SCREENSHOT?
AH!
KASHA (CLICK) カシャ
AH.
KASHA カシャ
AH...
KASHA カシャ
OH MAAAN! I'M HAPPY FOR YOU.
IT WAS DEFINITELY WORTH CHEERING YOU ON.
PACHI パチ
PACHI (CLAP) パチ
PACHI パチ
THAT'S GREAT!

I HAVE HIM...!
MY FAVORITE CHARACTER IS ON MY PHONE...!

I GOT HIM!!!!
WHAT ARE YOU DOIN' OVER THERE?
BE CAREFUL GOIN' HOME, NOW.

Do You Like the Nerdy Nurse?

Do You Like the Nerdy Nurse?

STRETCHER, CHECK.
AED, CHECK.
FIRST AID KIT, CHECK.
BAN (BAM)
Chapter 9:
98% Compatibility!!
BANNER: FIRST AID STATION
AS MEMBERS OF THE PUBLIC HEALTH COMMITTEE, LET'S COMBINE OUR EFFORTS...
ZAWA (CHATTER)
...TO GET THROUGH THIS SITUATION!
ZAWA
三津木中学校
救護所
S-SO...
AHEM...
BANNER: MITSUGI MIDDLE SCHOOL

......
M...
MEMBERS.
BA (FWIP)
ばっ
護所
R...
REPORT TO YOUR STATIONS ...
SHIN (SILENCE)
しん…
PURU
プル
PURU (QUIVER)
プル
救護
OKAY.
DIS-MISSED.
YES, MA'AM.
ZORO (BUZZ)
ぞろ
PAN (CLAP)
パン
PAN
パン
PAN
パン
ZORO
ぞろ

三津
救護所
SIGH...
MOMO-YAMA-SENSEI.
WERE YOU TRYING TO DO SOMETHING THERE?
HUH...?
AH...
K-KIND OF.
I WAS THINKING OF SHINKALION'S...
...TRANS-CEIVER, AND SUDDENLY...
DIRECTOR HAYASUGI'S COOL POSE?
BISHI (FWISH)
THAT'S THE ONE!
ISN'T SHINKALION GREAT...?
THEY STICK TO THE CLASSIC TROPES...
AND MORE THAN ANYTHING, THE ADULTS AND KIDS IN THE SHOW ARE ALL CUTE!
THEY ALSO THROW IN A BUNCH OF REFERENCES FOR OLDER ANIME FANS TO ENJOY...
THE MAIN CHARACTER IS AN ELEMENTARY SCHOOL STUDENT. AHHH...
OH.
?

IN BACK.
MAY I?
HUH?
YOUR KNOT IS VERTICAL.
TSUN (POKE)
つん
KYU (TUG)
きゅ
THERE YOU GO.

TH- THANK YOU.
DON'T GET HURT, NOW.
SEE YOU LATER.
S...
SEE YOU...!

入場門
BANNER: ENTRANCE
ワァァァ
WAAA (SHOUT)
ワァ WAA
ワァ WAA
NEXT CLASS, GATHER OVER HERE!
三津木中学
救護所
IT LOOKS PEACEFUL OVER AT THE FIRST AID STATION.
ごくり
GOKURI (GULP)

ZA (CHFF)
ザッ
BUT FROM HERE ON IN...
ZA
ザッ
ZA
ザッ
...THIS'LL BECOME THE PUBLIC HEALTH COMMITTEE'S BATTLEFIELD.
ZA
ザッ
WAAAA
ワアアアア
The next event...
...is the cavalry battle!!
GATA (RATTLE)
ガタ
WAAA
ワア
WAAA
ワア
MOMOYAMA-SENSEI...
THIS IS HER FIRST CAVALRY BATTLE HERE.

WH...
WHOA!
MITSUGI MIDDLE SCHOOL'S INFAMOUS EVENT...
THE CAVALRY BATTLE!!
FOR SOME REASON, CURRENT AND FORMER MITSUGI STUDENTS GET REALLY, REALLY INTO THIS.
AND EVERY YEAR, THERE ARE INEVITABLY SEVERAL CASUALTIES.
AS A MEMBER OF THE PUBLIC HEALTH COMMITTEE, I WISH THEY WOULD CANCEL THIS EVENT.

Ready...
PAAN (BLAM)
WAAAA (SHOUT)
DO
DO
DO
DO (DUN)
NOT GOOD AT FIGHTING
ARMBAND: PUBLIC HEALTH COMMITTEE
CARRY THE WOUNDED OFF THE FIELD!
WAA
WAA
THE TENT ALONE AIN'T GONNA CUT IT!
TAKE 'EM TO THE NURSE'S OFFICE!
WAA

ZURAAA (PACKED)
THIS MANY...
WHAT IS THIS, A CLASS PHYSICAL EXAM!?
MOMO-CHAN-SENSEI!
WE'VE GOT ANOTHER ONE.
BRING HIM IN.
AT A TIME LIKE THIS...
...IF ONLY THERE WAS A COMMITTEE MEMBER HERE WITH 98% COMPATIBILITY ...
GAGA (CRACKLE)
COMPATI-BILITY...?
MOMO-YAMA-SENSEI.
I'M BACK FROM THE COMPETITION.
WAA (SHOUT)
WAA
WHAT'S THE SITUATION IN THE NURSE'S OFFICE?

THE PUBLIC HEALTH COMMITTEE MEMBER WITH 98% COMPATI-BILITY!!
Huh? What?
Ah!
There's someone out here who can't move.
Can I carry him over to you?
BA (FWIP)
KURITA-KUN!

MOVE OUT...
...WITH THE STRETCHER !!
I'LL PUT THE STRETCHER BACK.
MOVE OUT WITH THE STRETCHER !!
BIKU (TWITCH)
I WAS SO BUSY, I DON'T QUITE REMEMBER...
...BUT I HAVE THE FEELING I SAID THAT.
BUT THE STUDENTS GOT INTO IT, SO I GUESS IT'S OKAY.

Do You Like
the Nerdy
Nurse?

Do You Like the Nerdy Nurse?

Chapter 10: aka Ishi-Blades

BANNER: ENTRANCE
入場門
KYUUU
(SQUEEZE)
きゅ〜う

I'M BACK.
MOMOYAMA-SENSEI?
UU
UUN (GROAN)
PATA
PATA (FLAIL)
AH!
OH!
GABA (SWISH)
KURITA-KUN!?
YOU LOOK LIKE...
...SOMETHING'S TROUBLING YOU.
A-ACTUALLY...
...I BROUGHT...
...SOME CHEERING ITEMS.
HUH?
SENSEI, YOU'LL CHEER US ON?
......

UM...
GOSO (RUSTLE)
IT'S THIS...
PIKA (FLICKER)
ISHIN ☆ LIVE...
...2.5-DIMENSIONAL...
*ACTORS AND VOICE ACTORS PORTRAY AND SING AS TWO-DIMENSIONAL CHARACTERS.
...CONCERT MERCH.
AKA...
...ISHI-BLADES.

THE LIGHT...
...CAN CHANGE TO TWELVE DIFFERENT COLORS, SO I THOUGHT I COULD CHEER ON ALL FIVE CLASSES THIS WAY.
ISHIN☆LIVE HAS MANY CHARACTERS AND GROUPS, SO I'M GRATEFUL FOR THIS COLOR-SWITCHING FUNCTION.
HUH, THAT'S COOL!
PA (FLASH)
PA
KACHI (CLICK)
KACHI
JAKIN (FWISH)
ISHIN LIVE
HANPEITA TAKECHI
ISHIN LIVE
IZOU OKADA
UM...
SO IF YOU DON'T MIND...
...I'VE GOT A FEW. WANNA BORROW ONE...?
BIKAAA (FLICKER)
OOH, IT REALLY CAN CHANGE INTO LOTS OF COLORS.
BUT WHY DO YOU HAVE SO MANY?
?
GIKU (ULP)

......
INEVITABILITY OF FATE...?
IF THERE ARE MULTIPLE DESIGNS, I WANT THEM ALL...
OH YEAH. THE DESIGNS ARE DIFFERENT.
...AND WHEN I GO, I ALWAYS BUY.
WHEN YOU GO?
FOR A CONCERT TOUR...
...I GO AS OFTEN AS POSSIBLE.
TOKYO
DAY 1 **/**
DAY 2 **/**
OSAKA
DAY 1 **/**
DAY 2 **/**
はっ
HA (GASP)
HAVING MULTIPLE ISHI-BLADES...
...COMES IN HANDY AT A TIME LIKE THIS.
I GET TO BORROW ONE!
YAY!

The next event...
...is the class relay race.
三津木中学校
BUT I BROUGHT THESE ISHI-BLADES FOR ANOTHER REASON...
...BESIDES THE COLORS ...
GATA (RATTLE)
I-IF THE SONG THEY PLAY...
DOKI
DOKI
DOKI (BADUM)
...FOR THIS RELAY IS THE SAME ONE THEY USED DURING PRACTICE...!
On your marks, get set...

PAAN (BLAM)
WAAAAA (ROAR)
CHANCHA (JANGLE)
CHANCHA
SENSEI, THIS SONG...
ISHIN ☆ LIVE
COM-BINED GROUPS SONG

THE BAKUMATSU ACADEMY IDOL DEVELOPMENT GAME, *ISHIN☆LIVE*...
...TAKES HISTORICAL FIGURES FROM THE BAKUMATSU ERA AS A MOTIF.
EACH CHARACTER HAS HIS OWN INDIVIDUAL AMBITION...
...SO THEIR COMBINED GROUP SONG...
...HAS SIMPLE LYRICS...
...AND IS UPLIFTING TO ANYONE WHO HAS A GOAL OF THEIR OWN!
DA
DA
DA.
DA. (DASH)
DA
...!
......!

THEIR YOUTH...
...SHINES LIKE A STAR.
SEN-SEI.
YOUR MOVEMENTS ARE SMALL.
AT THE CONCERT VENUE...
...THE IRON-CLAD RULE IS...
...PEN-LIGHTS AND FANS HAVE TO BE...
...KEPT AT CHEST LEVEL.

Do You Like
the Nerdy
Nurse?

Do You Like the Nerdy Nurse?

ZAAAA
(FSHHH)
ザアアアア
Chapter 11:
Because You Can't Share When You're Alone
KOCHI
(TICK)
コチ
KOCHI
コチ
KOCHI
コチ
KOCHI
コチ
IT'S...
...A LITTLE WET.
I CAN'T GO...
...TO THE NURSE'S OFFICE TODAY.

I'LL BE COMING HOME LATE. MAKE SOMETHING FOR YOURSELF AGAIN. SORRY THE PLACE IS A MESS! MOM
カチャ
KACHA (CLATTER)
カチャ
KACHA
ジャー…
JAAAA (SZZZ)
ガコッ
GAKO (CLUNK)

ZAAAAA (SSSS)
ザァァァ
BATAN (CHAK)
バタン
KARAN (JINGLE)
カラン
ZAKU (CHOP)
ザク
ZAKU
ザク
KOTSU (CLACK)
コッ
KOTSU
コッ

BWA-HA-HA!
MOGU (CHEW)
もぐ
MOGU
もぐ
IT'S HARD TO JUST MAKE ENOUGH ...
...FOR ONE PERSON.
IT TURNED OUT PRETTY WELL...
...SO I HOPE SHE EATS IT.

KOCHI (TICK) コチ
KOCHI コチ
コチ KOCHI
KOCHI コチ
COME TO THINK OF IT...
...LAST NIGHT WAS THE FINAL EPISODE OF ISHIN ☆ LIVE...
POCHI (CLICK) ポチ
ポチ POCHI
I was impressed...
Could you feel his presence...?
He seemed familiar somehow...
The legendary alum...
Nariakira Shimazu...
Wait...
It can't be...

DAN (DUN)
See you NEXT STAGE!!
THEY'RE GONNA...
...HAVE A SECOND SEASON!
MOMO-YAMA-SENSEI ...
...MUST BE THRILLED ABOUT THAT.
TSU (SWIPE)
TSU
TSU
19:32
Talk deck

19:32
@mertwa_otjg
@t_momomomo_t ··· One day ago
Executed
next stage
@t_momomomo_t ··· One day ago
Executed
something to live for
@t_momomomo_t ··· One day ago
Executed
master...master...
('ω')ノ @eiatwp
YUP.
SHE SEEMS HAPPY.
A SERIES OF POSTS IN ALL LOWER-CASE WITH BARELY ANY PUNC-TUATION.
IT'S HARD TO RESPOND TO ANY OF THESE...
POCHI (CLICK)
ポチ
POCHI
ポチ
FOR NOW, I'LL JUST "LIKE" THEM...
I CAN'T WAIT TILL TOMORROW.

PIYO (CHIRP)
ピヨ
PIYO
ピヨ
GAKO (CLUNK)
ガコッ
CARTON: FARM
PATAN (SHUT)
パタ――
牧場
OH WELL...
SEE YOU LATER.
BATAN (SHP)
バタン

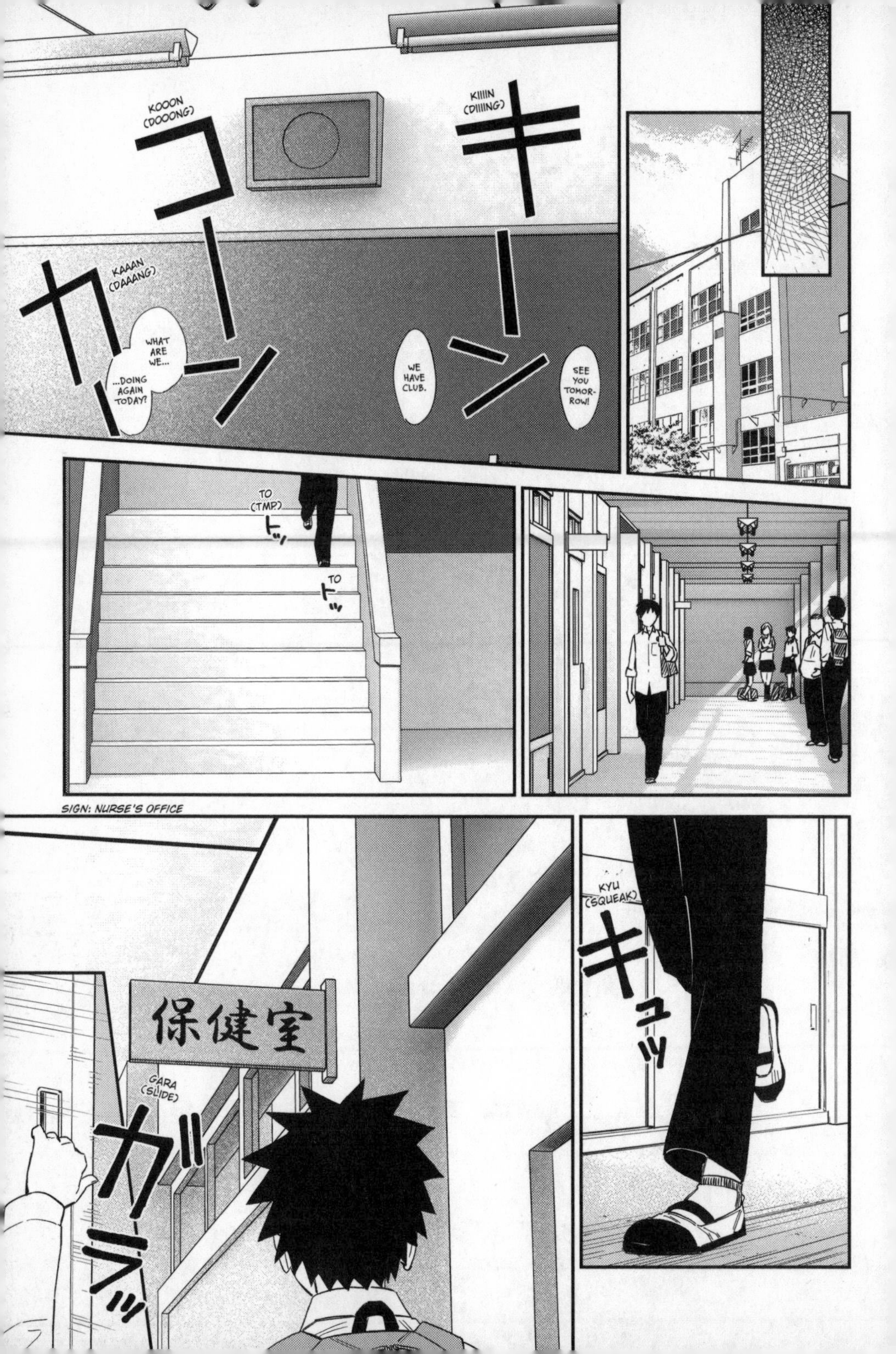

KIIIN (DIIIING)
KOOON (DOOONG)
KAAAN (DAAANG)
SEE YOU TOMORROW!
WE HAVE CLUB.
WHAT ARE WE...
...DOING AGAIN TODAY?
TO (TMP)
TO
SIGN: NURSE'S OFFICE
KYU (SQUEAK)
保健室
GARA (SLIDE)

BOOO (DAAAZE)
ボ"

WHA ...!?
OH.
BIKU (TWITCH)
ビクッ
WEL-COME.
KATAKATA (CLACK)
カタカタ
KACHI (CHIK)
カチカチッ
KACHI
KATAKATA
カタカタ
(I'M WORKING, SEE?)
KATAKATA
カタカタ
KATAKATA
カタカタ
KACHI
カチッ
I'LL GET US SOME TEA.
TH-THANK YOU.

YOU SEEM...
...UNEASY ABOUT SOMETHING.
YES.
I.
SO.
AAAM!
"THANK YOU FOR DOING A SECOND SEASON!"
I MEAN FOR ISHILI, BUT...
*SHORT FOR ISHIN☆LIVE
SURE, I UNDERSTAND.

THAT WAS BUILDING UP SINCE LAST NIGHT, SO I'M GLAD I HAD THE CHANCE...
...TO GET IT OFF MY CHEST.
AHHHH...

BECAUSE...
...YOU CAN'T SHARE...
...WHEN YOU'RE ALONE.
...YEAH.
THAT'S RIGHT.

THERE'S SOCIAL MEDIA...
...BUT IT JUST BUILDS UP UNLESS I CAN GET IT ALL OUT TALKING LIKE THIS.
FACE-TO-FACE...
UH, I MEAN, MY JOB IS TO...
...LISTEN TO PEOPLE, SO...
SENSEI.
I...
WHEN I...
...GET TO LISTEN TO YOU TALK...

...I LOVE IT.
...HUH?
OH...
THANK YOU...?
IF YOU DON'T MIND, KURITA-KUN...
YOU...

DOKIN (BADUMP)
ドキン
......
......?
DOKIN
ドキン
DOKIN
ドキン

Do You Like the Nerdy Nurse?

BONUS
BII (RIP)
NOOOO! IT HAPPENED AGAIN...
TEEEN (TA-DAAA)
LUCKILY, I THOUGHT TO HAVE A SPARE PAIR OF STOCKINGS ON HAND.
A TRICK I LEARNED SINCE I STARTED WORKING!
I'M PROUD OF MYSELF!
NO ONE IS AROUND...
...SO HERE IS FINE!
SHA (SWISH)

HELLO!
AAAAAAH!!
WAIT A SEC!
WAIT...
SHA
THANK YOU FOR WAITING!
ZURI (SLIP)
SENSEI, I-I THINK YOU NEED TO FIX YOUR SKIRT...
WHA ...!?
TH-THIS IS LIKE A TYPICAL LUCKY PERV MOMENT...!
SORRY ABOUT THAT!
WHEN UPSET, SHE GOES INTO FULL OTAKU MODE.

THE END

IZOU-CHAN WOULD NEVER HAVE A BUTT LIKE THIS!!!!
MOMO-YAMA-SENSEI
PA (PAT)
PA

ISHIN☆LIVE

イシン☆ライブ

YOUNG MEN WHO HAVE INHERITED THE MEMORIES OF IMPERIAL LOYALIST SAMURAI OF THE BAKUMATSU ERA EXCHANGE THEIR SWORDS FOR MICROPHONES AND SHOUT OUT THEIR FEELINGS! IT'S A BAKUMATSU SCHOOL IDOL DEVELOPMENT GAME.

...IS THE BASIC SETUP.

IZOU OKADA

KNOWN AS "MANSLAYER IZOU" AND "THE IRON NOMAD" IN THE BAKUMATSU ERA.

HIS SWORDSMANSHIP SKILL HAS NOW BECOME HIS SINGING SKILL. THE ONLY THING HE KNOWS HOW TO DO IS GRAB A MIC AND SHOUT IT ALL OUT.

IN THE PRESENT, NO ONE ABANDONS OR BEHEADS HIM.

TENDS TO THINK OF HIMSELF AS USELESS.

PLEASED WHEN PEOPLE RELY ON HIM.
ACTS COOL, BUT IS PRETTY CHILDISH.

HANPEITA TAKECHI

THE DOJO "TEACHER" OF THE BAKUMATSU ERA, LEADER OF THE TOSA IMPERIALISM PARTY.

HONEST, SERIOUS, GOOD AT BOTH ACADEMICS AND SPORTS.
ENJOYS DRAWING.

EVEN NOW, PASSIONATE ABOUT EDUCATION, IS STRICT ABOUT LESSONS TO THE PEOPLE AROUND HIM (ESPECIALLY TO IZOU).

IZOU IS LIKE FAMILY TO HIM, BUT HIS FEELINGS FOR IZOU ARE COMPLICATED. RYOUMA SAYS, "YOU GUYS ARE A PAIN."

MOMO-CHAN-SENSEI'S FAVORITE!

☆ SPECIAL THANKS ☆
MY EDITOR, THE DESIGNER, MY ASSISTANTS, MY FRIENDS, AND THE READERS.

Do You Like the Nerdy Nurse?

MIIIN (KRIK)
MIN
MIII
Chapter 12:
Summer Anime Are About to Start...
CAN: CITRUS

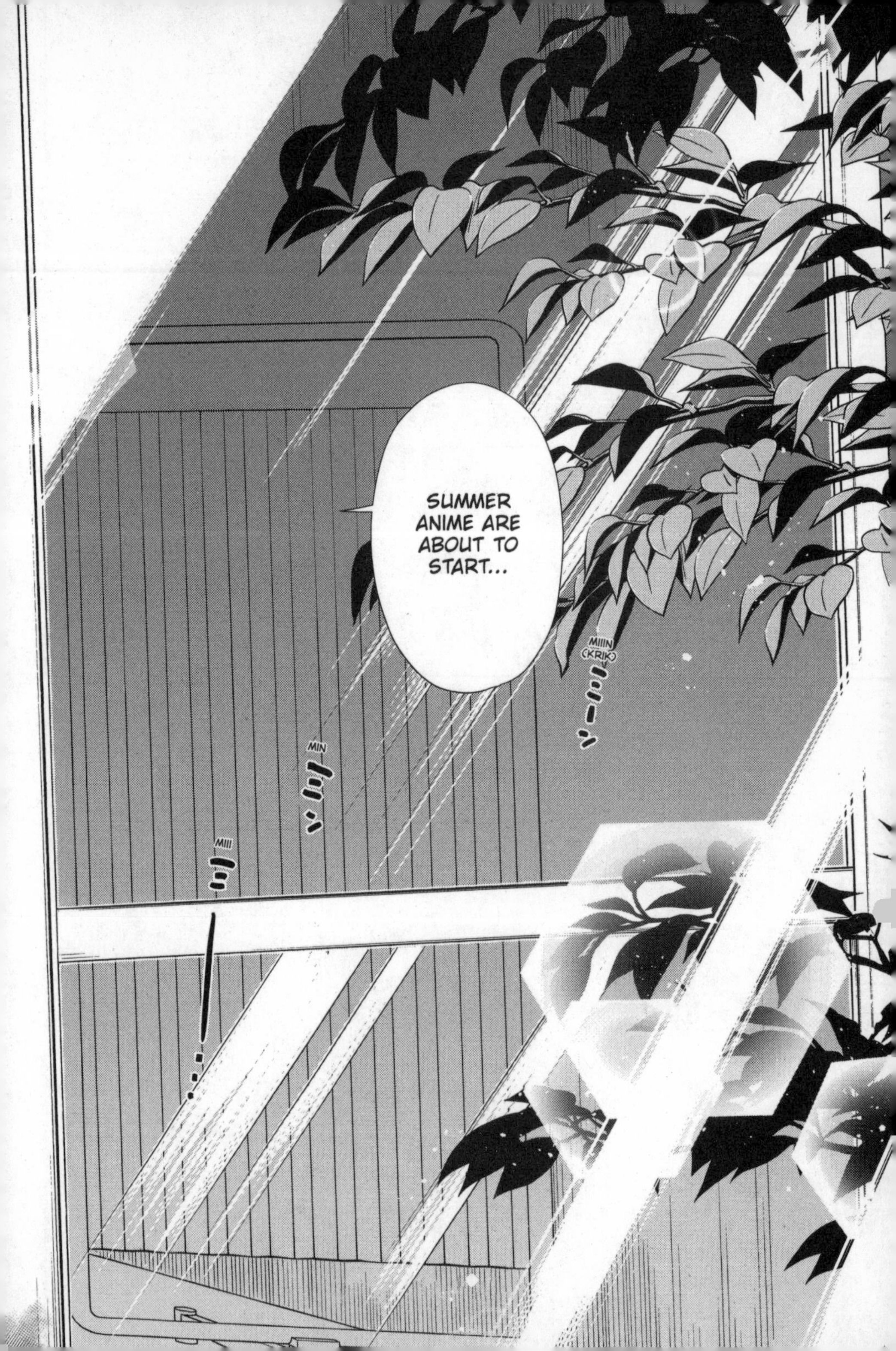
SUMMER ANIME ARE ABOUT TO START...
MIIIN (KRIK)
MIN
MIII

FEELS LIKE TIME'S GOING BY TOO FAST.

AH.
THAT'S YUZUKI.
MAN, HE'S FAST.
YUZUKI...
DUDE, YOU CAN REALLY RUN.
YEAH, I GUESS.
YOU GUESS!?
MAYBE IF I PUSHED MYSELF...

EVEN IN MIDDLE SCHOOL, PEOPLE MAKE A BIG DEAL OUT OF FAST RUNNERS.
YEAH, BUT YUZUKI-KUN IS AN ALL-AROUND ATHLETE.
NOT ONLY THAT. HE'S SERIOUS AND GETS GOOD GRADES TOO.
IT'S LIKE HE CAN DO ANYTHING.
RUNNING FAST IS THE ICING ON THE CAKE.
AH HA HA!
AS LONG AS I DON'T HAVE TO COMPETE AGAINST HIM!
I WISH I WAS AS CAREFREE AS YOU, KURITA.

UGH, I CAN'T STOP SWEATING.
PATA (FAN) ぱた
PATA ぱた
WANT A WIPE?
THANKS.
DOKA (BUMP) ドカッ
OH, SORRY.
YUZUKI-KUN...
PATA (FWAP) パタッ
HUH? YOU DROPPED SOME-THING.

地上に舞い降りた最強月姫の
剣戟アクション
江山鶩
AHIRU EYAMA
MANGA: SENGOKU MOON PRINCESS MIKAZUKI VOLUME 1 BY AHIRU EYAMA / THE MIGHTY MOON PRINCESS WHO CAME TO EARTH'S SWASHBUCKLING ACTION
I'VE NEVER HEARD OF THIS MANGA.
BUT IT LOOKS COOL.
THANK YOU.
YUZUKI-KUN READS MANGA.
AND, NOT A MAJOR SERIES...
I'M KIND OF SURPRISED...

保健室
SIGN: NURSE'S OFFICE
キーン
KIIN (DIIING)
コーン
KOOON (DOOONG)
カーン
KAAAN (DAAANG)
THE NURSE'S OFFICE..
はた
HATA (FAN)
はた
HATA
...IS NICE AND COOL.
I'D BETTER START GETTING READY FOR FINALS.
IT'S. ALWAYS NOISY AT MY HOUSE, SO IT'S HARD TO STUDY.
WELL, YOU CAN'T JUST HANG OUT AT THE NURSE'S OFFICE AFTER SCHOOL.
AH...
HEY, LISTEN ...
MY PLACE...
...IS PRETTY EMPTY UNTIL LATE...
...SO IF YOU WANNA STUDY...
FOR REAL? MAYBE I'LL TAKE YOU UP ON THAT.
!
YOU SHOULD.

WILL YOU STUDY TOGETHER?
OH... SURE.
I SEE...
STUDYING WITH A FRIEND IS MORE FUN.
THAT'S NICE.
I BET YOU'VE GOT A TON OF MANGA AT YOUR HOUSE, KURITA.
REMEMBER, THE IDEA IS TO STUDY...
KON (KNOCK)
KON

EXCUSE ME.
GARA (RATTLE)
I'M KENGO YUZUKI, A SECOND-YEAR.
I WAS RUNNING DURING CLUB AND TWISTED MY ANKLE.
UNIFORM: MITSUGI
HUH? YUZUKI-KUN.
HERE, HAVE A SEAT.
GOTO (CLUNK)
I SEE. SO YOU'RE AN ASSISTANT HERE, KURITA-KUN?
REFRESHING AURA
YEAH...

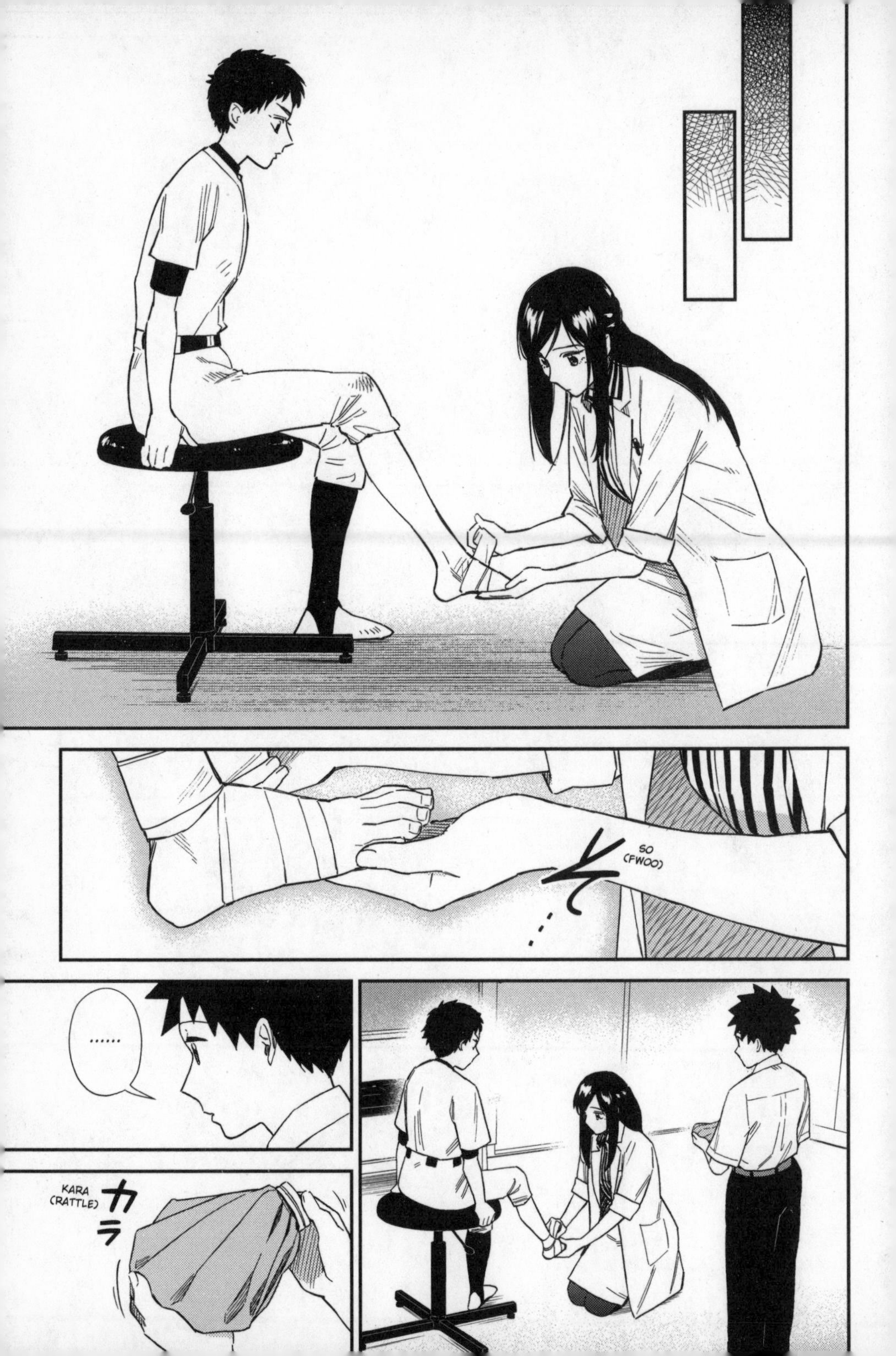
ソ
SO (FWOO)
...
......
カラ
KARA (RATTLE)

SOWA (FIDGET)
そわ
SOWA
そわ
HUH, THIRD BASE.
A HEROIC POSITION.
DO YOU LIKE BASEBALL, SENSEI?
OH...JUST BASEBALL MANGA, A LITTLE...
I FOLLOW THEM FOR THE CHARACTERS. I DON'T REALLY KNOW THE RULES OF THE GAME...
WELL, IF IT'S MANGA...
KIRA (GLITTER)
キラ
...IT'S PROBABLY INTERESTING ...
...BECAUSE OF THE CHARACTERS.
KIRA
キラ
OH? YUZUKI-KUN...
...DO YOU READ MANGA ...?
THAT EXPLANATION...

I'M A PRETTY AVID READER.
RECENTLY...
WHAT KIND OF MANGA DO YOU LIKE TO READ?
......!
ZUI (LEAN)
KARA (RATTLE)

PA (FWAH)
ぱっ
I TOTALLY JUST CUT IN...!
M...
MOMO-YAMA-SENSEI...!
WHAT DO YOU LIKE...
...ABOUT BASEBALL MANGA?
W...
WELL, LET'S SEE...
I'D SAY... THE CHARM OF THE CHARACTER RELATIONSHIPS ...
KIRI (GLINT)
FRIENDSHIP, CAMARA-DERIE...
ANTAGONISM AND STRATEGY...
SWEAT AND TEARS...

IT'S LIKE I WANT TO BE THE MOM OF ONE OF THOSE BOYS...
...AND WATCH OVER HIM.
AS...
...IF.
......

BUT REALLY ...
...I LOVE KIDS...
...SO THAT'S WHY I'M A SCHOOL NURSE!
SCHOOL NURSE
NIJIKO MOMOYAMA
MITSUGI MIDDLE SCHOOL
SHARARAN (GLEAM)
SA (SHF)
HER VOICE IS BARELY A WHISPER ...!!

THAT KIND OF MANGA MAKES ME WANNA CHEER THE CHARACTERS ON TOO.
AHHH! I FEEL LIKE I TRIED TO COVER FOR MYSELF WHEN I DIDN'T EVEN NEED TO...
CAN'T KEEP UP WITH THE DYNAMIC

I WAS SURPRISED TO LEARN MOMO-CHAN-SENSEI IS AN OTAKU...
...BUT YUZUKI CAN TALK MANGA TOO, HUH?
......
I...
...KNEW IT ALREADY.

TSUN (TUG)
KURITA...
YOU'RE...
...IN LOVE WITH MOMO-CHAN-SENSEI, AREN'T YOU?

Do You Like the Nerdy Nurse?

Do You Like
the Nerdy
Nurse?

CHARI (JINGLE)
Chapter 13:
Acquire Info and Luck!
GURAAA (RUMBLE)
MAIN DISH
FRIED NOODLES
ROLL
RANK DOWN
BY SAVING UP MY LUNCH MONEY...
...I FINALLY HAVE JUST OVER 400 YEN.
*BASICALLY, STUDENTS BRING THEIR OWN LUNCHES AT MITSUGI MIDDLE SCHOOL, BUT THERE ARE DAYS WHEN THE SCHOOL SELLS BAKED GOODS.
IN ORDER TO BUY THE SPECIAL EDITION OF THE GAME I WANT...
PP4 VIDEO GAME
MAKING OF THE GAME
SOUND-TRACK
...I NEED ANOTHER 3,500 YEN.
I LOVE THIS SERIES, SO I'M WILLING TO SUFFER TILL I CAN GET THE SPECIAL EDITION...
GURARAAA
TOBO (PLOD)
TOBO
IS THERE A WAY I CAN MAKE MORE MONEY?
SIGN: NURSE'S OFFICE
保健室
......

HMMM...
......
AS THE SCHOOL NURSE...
GUUUU (RUMBLE)
...I CAN'T RECOMMEND...
...SAVING YOUR LUNCH MONEY.
YEAH, I KNOW...
SHOBO (MOPE)
BUT...
...I TOTALLY UNDERSTAND WHERE YOU'RE COMING FROM!
KA (FLASH)

LET'S SEE...
SUCHA (FWIP)
GLASSES FOR COMPUTER USE
...WHAT WE CAN DO!!
GATA (RATTLE)
...!?
O...
OKAY...!
THE GOAL IS SAVING UP MONEY...
MAYBE THE FASTEST WAY...
...OF RAISING MONEY...
...WOULD BE TO SELL THINGS.
LIKE OLD BOOKS?

IT WOULD BE A WASTE...
...TO JUST SELL THINGS RANDOM-LY!!
ZUN CLEAN
AC-QUIRE...
...INFO AND LUCK!
MERA (BLAZE)
INFO...
...AND LUCK...
KOKU
KOKU (NOD)
THESE DAYS, THERE ARE MANY...
...SPECIALTY SHOPS THAT PAY WELL...
...FOR OLDER ITEMS.
FOR EXAMPLE, SOMETHING THAT SOLD FOR 3,000 YEN OR LESS WHEN ITS ASSOCIATED ANIME WAS ON THE AIR...
THINGS RELATED TO THE ANIME VERSION OF FATE ARE GOING UP IN VALUE THANKS TO FGO'S POPULARITY.
...NOW GOES FOR 10,000 YEN.
THAT'S JUST ONE EXAMPLE.

AND THAT'S NOT ALL.
DEPENDING ON THE PERSON (SHOP)...
...THE VALUE OF THE ITEM CAN CHANGE.
こあーと中野店2号館
MONEY EXCHANGE
CD・DVD
ブルーレイ
Pitakora Toys for Adults Shop Pickup Buying/Selling Chart
SIGNS: (LEFT): COMICS, ANIME, GAMES / WE BUY AND SELL CDS, DVDS, BLU-RAYS / COAATO STORE #1 (TOP): COAATO NAKANO STORE #2 MERCHANDISE
DEPENDING ON WHAT THAT STORE IS COLLECTING...
STORE THAT SELLS MERCH APPEALING TO FEMALES
HIGHER PRICES
ITEM RELATED TO A CERTAIN PROPERTY
STORE THAT SELLS MERCH APPEALING TO MALES
LOWER PRICES
...THE AMOUNT THEY'RE WILLING TO BUY AND SELL FOR CHANGES.
ONCE IN A WHILE...
...SOMETHING WILL BE SELLING FOR A HIGH PRICE, AND YOU'LL BE LIKE...
..."WHY THIS?"
SO CHECK OUT THE SHOPS VEEERY CAREFULLY.
END OF IMPASSIONED SPEECH
SORRY. I WAS TALKING TOO FAST...
I'LL DO MY BEST!!

SIGNS: COAATO STORE #3 / MANTENYA SPECIAL BUILDING

FIRST, I'LL GET AN OVERVIEW...
3
¥5.000
¥4.500
ANTENYA SPECIAL 3
CERTAINLY...
...THE PRICES DO DIFFER FROM STORE TO STORE.
BUT IT WOULD BE TOUGH TO COMPARE EVERYTHING...
KYORO (GLANCE)
キョロ
KYORO
キョロ
SIGN: COAATO STORE #4
THE DOLL I SAW GOING FOR 1,800 YEN OVER THERE...
WOW!
...SELLS FOR 5,000 YEN HERE!!
THIS IS...
...KIND OF FUN.

...
THIS MOVIE'S BONUS FILM STRIP...
I BROUGHT THAT WITH ME.
I DON'T MIND HAVING IT...
...BUT I NEVER FIGURED OUT WHAT TO DO WITH IT.
PERA (FLIP)
LABEL: BASE PRICE (EXCLUDING TAX)
本体
（税別）
¥45,000
FORTY-FIVE THOUSAND YEN!?!?!?

HUH!? THIS!? WHY!?
AH, BUT DEPENDING ON WHAT IT IS, THE PRICE IS COMPLETELY DIFFERENT.
WHAT'S THE DIFFERENCE!?
DOKI (BADUMP)
ONCE IN A WHILE...
...SOMETHING WILL BE SELLING FOR A HIGH PRICE, AND YOU'LL BE LIKE...
DOKI
DOKI
..."WHY THIS?"
SO CHECK OUT THE SHOPS VEEERY CAREFULLY.
DOKI
DOKI
O-OKAY, CALM DOWN.
UM, SHE SAID...
...THEY BUY FOR ANYWHERE BETWEEN A THIRD AND HALF OF WHAT THEY SELL IT FOR, SO...
...HOW MUCH...
...WOULD I GET FOR THIS?

まんてんや買取処
SIGN: MANTENYA BUY COUNTER
WE CAN PAY YOU TEN THOUSAND YEN...
...FOR THAT.
TEN...
...THOUSAND!?!?!?
DARA (DRIP)
DARA
ダラ
ダラ

DO YOU HAVE A GUARDIAN RELEASE FORM?
HUH?
FOR MINORS...
...WE REQUIRE A GUARDIAN RELEASE FORM...
...AND A PARENT'S OR GUARDIAN'S I.D.
GUARDIAN RELEASE FORM
I AGREE TO SELL THIS ITEM TO MANTENYA, INC.
AGE
NAME
GUARDIAN
ADDRESS
PHONE #
MANTENYA
LIKE THIS

OH, I SEE... IT MAKES SENSE...
CAN I GET MOM TO SIGN THE RELEASE FORM?
IT'S HARD TO BRING UP MY HOBBIES WITH HER.
I CAN'T WAIT TO BECOME AN ADULT...
SU (SHFF)

M...
SA (FWISH)
MOMOYAMA-SENSEI...!?
THIS IS THE FIRST TIME...
...I'VE SEEN HER IN TOWN.
DOKI (BADUM)
DOKI
SA (SHF)
EX-CUSE ME...
DO YOU HAVE THIS IN STOCK?
...YES.
WE DO!
IS SHE GOING TO BUY SOMETHING?

THIS JUST...
...CAME IN.
WE HAVEN'T EVEN HAD TIME TO PUT THEM ON THE SHELVES YET.
YES, I SAW ON SOCIAL MEDIA JUST A LITTLE WHILE AGO THAT YOU GOT THEM IN...
...SO I WANTED TO COME BEFORE YOU SOLD OUT...
INFO AND LUCK...
SHE FOLLOWED THAT ADVICE HERE...!?
BEFORE THE ITEM COULD SELL OUT...
THAT DAY, KURITA-KUN...
...FELT LIKE HE SAW A TRUE WARRIOR STANDING ON THE BATTLEFIELD.
AMAZING... I'LL TRY TO GROW UP TO BE LIKE MOMOYAMA-SENSEI...!
THIS IS PRETTY MUCH THE LIST PRICE.
I SAW IT CHEAPER IN AKIHABARA...

Do You Like the Nerdy Nurse?

Do You Like the Nerdy Nurse?

Chapter 14: Which Love Is Right!?

DON
(BAM)

WHICH LOVE IS RIGHT!?
YOU CAN'T COMPARE THINGS LIKE THAT.
YOU'RE FRIENDS...
...WHICH IS ALL THE MORE REASON...
...TO ASK THE BOY YOU LIKE HOW HE FEELS...
...AND TRY TO FIND A WAY...
...TO BE AT PEACE WITH EACH OTHER AGAIN.
MOMOYAMA-SENSEI IS LECTURING...
WHAT ...?
IF WE COULD EASILY ASK YUZUKI-KUN...
...HOW HE FEELS...

HE LIVES...
...IN THIS WORLD!
IN FACT, HE'S IN THE SAME BUILDING...
...SO DO WHAT YOU CAN!!
SEN-SEI...
MOMO-CHAN...
MOMO-YAMA-SENSEI...

BECAUSE IF HE WERE IN ANOTHER DIMENSION...
...THEY WOULDN'T EVEN BE ABLE TO MEET HIM.
SENSEI, UM...THE PERSON YOU LOVE...DID THEY PASS AWAY...?
NO, BUT THEY'RE SO FAR AWAY THAT THEY'RE BEYOND MY REACH...
WHEN MOMOYAMA-SENSEI HAS HER "EDUCATOR SWITCH" ON...
...SHE BECOMES STEEL ON THE INSIDE.

DAYS LATER
ISHIN☆LIVE
Collaboration Menu

I MANAGED TO GET THIS TIE-IN CAFÉ EXCLUSIVE ...
...IZOU-CHAN ILLUSTRATED COASTER!!
I LOVE THE NOVELTY OF GETTING TO CHOOSE WHICH ONE.
MOMOYAMA-SENSEI'S FELLOW NERD FRIEND
WELL, IF IT WERE RANDOM, FOOD FIGHTS WOULD PROBABLY BREAK OUT.
THIS IS CAFÉ-STYLE IZOU-CHAN...
STRETCHING HER IMAGINATION
PAR-FET...
P-PAR-FAY...?
...BUT I WONDER IF HE'S ABLE TO WAIT TABLES.
YOU NEVER KNOW. MAYBE HE'S ACTUALLY REALLY GOOD AT IT.
AH HA HA!
FRIEND
IT'S JUST NOT IN HIS WHEELHOUSE. HE'D MESS UP, BUT IT WOULD BE CUTE.
JARA (KACLANG)
WOW, WHAT AN ITA-BAG...
AN IZOU-CHAN FAN.

EXCUSE ME...
FELLOW FAN...
...WOULD YOU MIND LEAVING?
? ? ? ? ? ? ? ? ? ? ? ? ? ?
IZOU-CHAN BELONGS TO ME...
ZAWA (CHATTER)
ZAWA
...SO, UM... A FELLOW FAN IS AN EYESORE...
W-WELL...

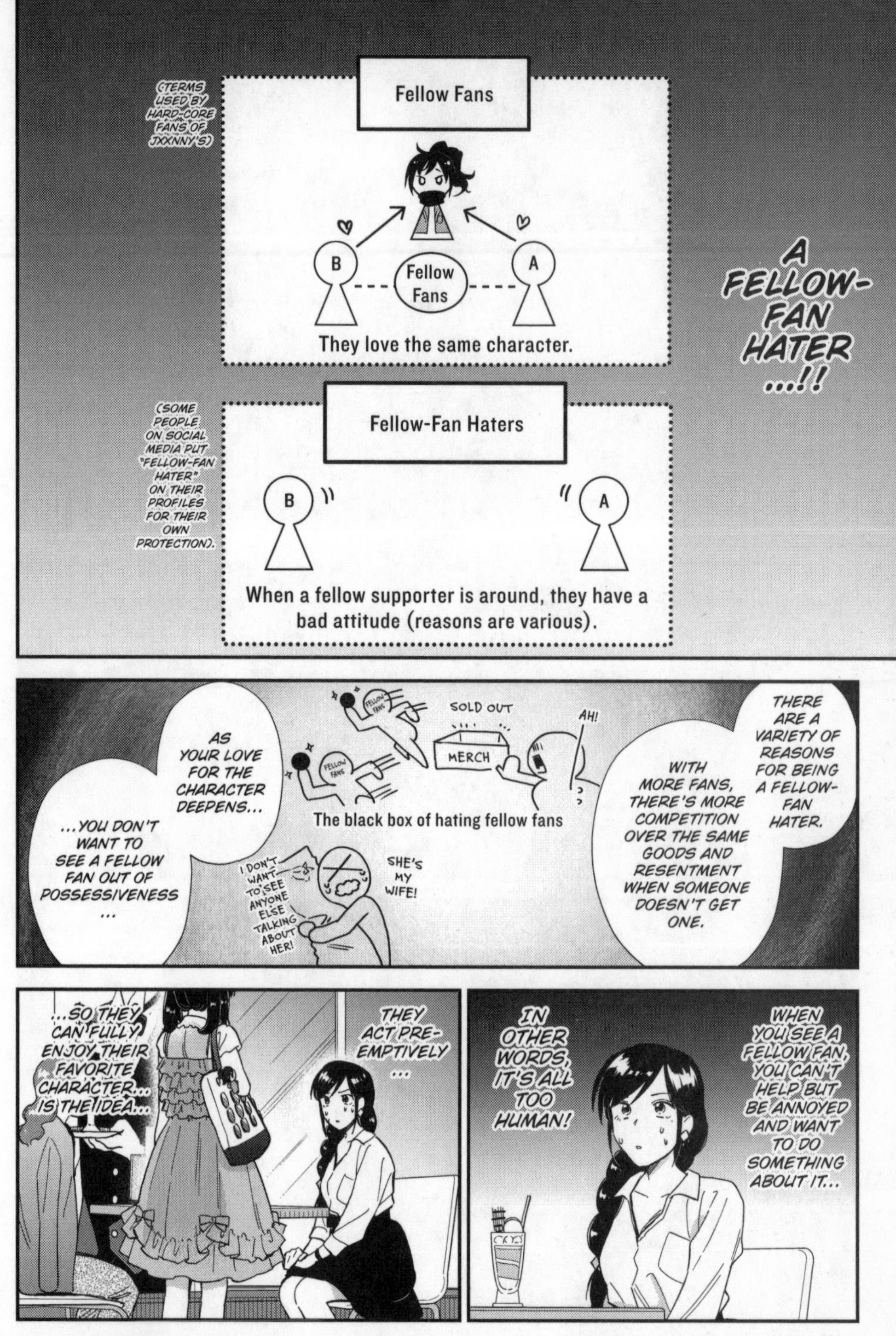

A FELLOW-FAN HATER ...!!
(TERMS USED BY HARD-CORE FANS OF JXXNNY'S)
Fellow Fans
B
Fellow Fans
A
They love the same character.
(SOME PEOPLE ON SOCIAL MEDIA PUT "FELLOW-FAN HATER" ON THEIR PROFILES FOR THEIR OWN PROTECTION).
Fellow-Fan Haters
B
A
When a fellow supporter is around, they have a bad attitude (reasons are various).
THERE ARE A VARIETY OF REASONS FOR BEING A FELLOW-FAN HATER.
WITH MORE FANS, THERE'S MORE COMPETITION OVER THE SAME GOODS AND RESENTMENT WHEN SOMEONE DOESN'T GET ONE.
SOLD OUT
MERCH
AH!
FELLOW FANS
FELLOW FANS
The black box of hating fellow fans
SHE'S MY WIFE!
I DON'T WANT TO SEE ANYONE ELSE TALKING ABOUT HER!
AS YOUR LOVE FOR THE CHARACTER DEEPENS...
...YOU DON'T WANT TO SEE A FELLOW FAN OUT OF POSSESSIVENESS ...
WHEN YOU SEE A FELLOW FAN, YOU CAN'T HELP BUT BE ANNOYED AND WANT TO DO SOMETHING ABOUT IT...
IN OTHER WORDS, IT'S ALL TOO HUMAN!
THEY ACT PRE-EMPTIVELY ...
...SO THEY CAN FULLY ENJOY THEIR FAVORITE CHARACTER... IS THE IDEA...

UM...
IF YOU ALREADY GOT THE PREMIUM, THEN YOU CAN MOVE ON, RIGHT?
GO (RUMBLE) GO
BUT THIS...
GO
...HAS GONE BEYOND...
GO GO
...FELLOW-FAN HATRED.
IT'S A THREAT!!
TH-THIS IS A PLACE WHERE PEOPLE WHO LIKE THE SAME CHARACTERS GATHER, SO...
LOVE THY NEIGHBOR! LOVE THY NEIGHBOR!
IT'S AN IMPOSSIBLE SITUATION WHEN TWO PEOPLE ARE IN LOVE WITH THE SAME PERSON, ISN'T IT?

YOU CAN'T SHARE A BOYFRIEND, HUSBAND, OR WIFE...
...CAN YOU?
COULD YOU ABIDE THAT?
IS THERE SOMETHING WRONG WITH YOU?
THERE ARE AS MANY FORMS OF LOVE AS THERE ARE PEOPLE.
UM, I'M WELL AWARE THAT THERE ARE FELLOW-FAN HATERS...
...BUT AT THE SAME TIME, THERE ARE PEOPLE WHO AREN'T LIKE THAT.
I LOVE IZOU-CHAN MORE THAN ANYONE!!
AND IZOU-CHAN LOVES ME!!

GATA
(RATTLE)

GATA (RATTLE)
ガタ
AH, EXCUSE ME.
MY APOLOGIES...
ZURU (SHIVER)
ズル
ZURU
ズル
ZURU
ズル
HARA (SHUDDER)
ハラ
...BUT COULD WE TRADE SEATS?
HARA
ハラ
SURE, FINE.
GATA
ガタ
ZURU
ズル
NOT EVERYONE...
THANK YOU!
...CAN GET ALONG. ☆

THE TWO GIRLS, LATER
YUZUKI-KUN IS OUR IDOL...
RIGHT.
...SO WHAT ABOUT GIVING HIM A SNACK?
DON'T BEAT ME TO THE PUNCH.
KURITA...
...WOULD YOU ASK YUZUKI-KUN HOW HE FEELS ABOUT US?
HUH!?

Do You Like the Nerdy Nurse?

Do You Like
the Nerdy
Nurse?

YUZUKI-KUN...
...BECAME A FREQUENT VISITOR AT THE NURSE'S OFFICE.
MIN
MIIIN (CHIRP)
MIII
MY OLDER SISTER MAKES HER OWN MANGA.
KATA (CLICK)
KATA
Chapter 15:
Would You Put That Talent to Work in the Nurse's Office?
SHE MAKES ME HELP HER A LOT.
PIKU (PERK)
PERA (RUSTLE)
AT FIRST, I WAS JUST PUTTING TOGETHER THE PHOTOCOPY BOOKS.
HER STORIES ARE USUALLY TWENTY TO THIRTY PAGES LONG, AND FIFTY AT THE MOST.
*PHOTOCOPY BOOKS: IN WHICH A COPY MACHINE MAKES PHOTOCOPIES OF A MANUSCRIPT, WHICH CAN THEN BE REPRODUCED AND FOLDED INTO A BOOK.
RECENTLY, SHE'S BEEN MAKING ME HELP HER WITH THE MANUSCRIPT, THOUGH...
...WHICH IS TOUGH.

YUZUKI-KUN!
CEREAL!?
GATA (RATTLE)
ガタッ
ARE YOU CEREAL !?
CE-REAL = SERI-OUS
Y-YES...
SHE GAVE ME AN IPAD...
...SO I PUT IN THE BACKGROUNDS AND STUFF.
LIKE A TREE OVER HERE...
I'LL USE A BRUSH FOR THE LEAVES...
...AND JUST DO A SIMPLE DRAWING.
SHA (SHIK)
シャッ
SHA
シャッ
H-HE'S GOOD...

YUZUKI-KUN...
WOULD YOU...
...PUT THAT TALENT...
...TO WORK IN THE NURSE'S OFFICE?
YOU TOO, KURITA-KUN!
I DON'T KNOW IF THE *HEALTH GAZETTE* IS GETTING THROUGH TO THE STUDENTS...
SUMMER VACATION IS COMING UP...
...SO THERE ARE A LOT OF DANGERS...
...LIKE HEAT-STROKE AND VIRUSES GOING AROUND.
MIDDLE SCHOOL STUDENTS HAVE A TENDENCY TO THINK OF THEMSELVES AS INVULNERABLE...
...SO I THINK MAYBE THEY NEED A STORY WITH PICTURES!

KURITA-KUN, YOU WRITE THE STORY...
...AND YUZUKI-KUN, YOU DO THE ART!
...UM—
TH-THAT'S WHAT I WAS THINKING ANYWAY...
I'LL DO IT!
GATA (RATTLE)

MOMOYAMA-SENSEI, JUST AS AN EXAMPLE...
...HOW ABOUT SOMETHING LIKE THIS?
No. 2
※ABOUT GETTING HEATSTROKE
DOKI
DOKI (BADUM)
JI (STARE)
DOKI
SINCE WE'RE DOING THIS...
...COULD YOU...
...GO BIGGER?
BIGGER...?

DANGERS CLOSING IN ON THE HUMAN BODY!
THE BOND BETWEEN FRIENDS!
AS TEMPERATURES ARE RISING, THE BATTLE WITH A VIRUS HEATS UP!

YOU KNOW CELLS AT WORK!, RIGHT?
O-OR SOMETHING...
ALONG THOSE LINES...
A NOBLE SACRIFICE AND A LESSON.
MY CELL MATE!
A SYMPA-THETIC HERO...
...AND A FIGHTING HEROINE.

THE BOYS' SPIRITS...
SA (SWF)
I NEED TO BORROW A BOOK!
...HAVE BEEN IGNITED.
THIS IS KIND OF MORE EXCITING THAN PLAYING BASEBALL...
YUZUKI-KUN...
WELL, YOU SHARE THE SAME BLOOD AS YOUR SISTER...
YUZUKI-KUN'S DRAWINGS ARE FIRST-CLASS...
...BUT I'VE BEEN A MEMBER OF THE PUBLIC HEALTH COMMITTEE FOR A LONG TIME.

IT WAS A CHALLENGE, BUT WHEN ALL IS SAID AND DONE...
...I'M HAPPY THAT YUZUKI-KUN'S TALENTED DRAWINGS...
...BROUGHT MY THOUGHTS TO LIFE...
CREATING SOMETHING TOGETHER...
I'LL ROTATE THIS STAPLER NINETY DEGREES ...!
IS THIS THE RIGHT ORDER?
...WAS A LOT OF FUN.
WE CAN USE COLORED STAPLES TOO...

AND IT'S DONE!!
保健だより
夏休みスペシャル
～灼熱の30日間～
COMIC: HEALTH GAZETTE / SUMMER VACATION SPECIAL - THIRTY DAYS OF RED-HOT ACTION!
WE PRINTED IT ON LARGE PAPER ...
...AND CUT IT ON THE CROP MARKS.
IT LOOKS LIKE IT JUST CAME OFF THE PRESSES!!
IF FOLDED, THE EDGES WON'T LINE UP...
...SO HE CUT THEM AND THEN LINED THEM UP.
THAT'S INCREDIBLE, YUZUKI-KUN!
ARE WE GOING TO MAKE ENOUGH FOR ALL THE STUDENTS IN THIS SCHOOL?
ABOUT 400 STUDENTS × 20 PAGES...

Do You Like
the Nerdy
Nurse?

Do You Like the Nerdy Nurse?

During summer vacation...
...please be careful...
...about what you eat and drink.
Chapter 16:
Cosplay Is More Than Just Wearing a Costume (Part One)
WHAT ARE YOU DOING OVER VACATION?
I'VE GOT CRAM SCHOOL EVERY DAY.
I CAN'T GO...
...TO THE NURSE'S OFFICE OVER THE SUMMER.
I WANT TO GO HOME...
...AS SOON AS I CAN.
EVEN WHEN YOU'RE INSIDE...
...TAKE MEASURES AGAINST HEAT-STROKE.
BECAUSE THERE'S SOME-THING...
...I NEED TO DO.

NOT LONG BEFORE THAT...
※ AFTER THE DOUJINSHI EVENT
MOMO...
HOW ABOUT WEARING A COSTUME?
HUH ...?
ME, COSPLAY?
NO, NO, NO, NO!
NO WAY, NO HOW!!
PAPER: ISHIN☆LIVE-ONLY DOUJIN EVENT
YOU COULD BE IZOU-CHAN...
...OR MAYBE IZOU-CHAN...
...OR EVEN IZOU-CHAN.
THAT WOULD BE PERFECT FOR YOU.
AND THEN, IF YOU WOULDN'T MIND, AT THE EVENT, WE COULD USE YOU TO DRAW IN CUSTOMERS AT OUR BOOTH...
YOU COULD LEAVE YOUR STUFF THERE TOO.
...JUST BY ROAMING AROUND THE VENUE AND HAVING FUN.
ISHIN☆LIVE

OH, I COULDN'T ...
ACTU-ALLY...
...SHE ISN'T TOTALLY OPPOSED TO THE IDEA.
BUT IF I'M GOING TO DO IT...
...I'D LIKE TO DO IT JUSTICE, EVEN IF IT'S JUST THIS ONCE.
YAY!!

AND SO...
...LITTLE BY LITTLE, SHE PREPARED TO COSPLAY.
LETTUCE
~MATERIALS~
~WIG~
~COLOR CONTACTS~
Color Contact lens
MOMOYAMA

SIGN: HIGH SCHOOL ENTRANCE EXAM HOPE

MOMO-YAMA-SENSEI...
...HOW ABOUT GOING TO LUNCH?
AH...
SORRY.
I HAVE PLANS...
SA (SHF)
SHE CAN'T...
TOO BAD...
SA
SA
SA
SA
SA
FULL-SPEED EXIT!!!
I'VE GOT THE COSTUME...
...BUT THERE ARE STILL A LOT OF OTHER THINGS LEFT TO DO!
COSPLAY...
...IS MORE THAN JUST WEARING A COSTUME!

ALL RIGHT!
ハ
サッ
PASA (FWAP)
THE FIGURE-CORRECTION CHALLENGE!!
どんっ
DON (BAM)
IZOU-CHAN IS A BOY...
...WITH A LEAN FIGURE!
IT WOULD BE PREPOSTEROUS TO JUST PUT ON THE COSTUME LIKE THIS!
laundry

THERE ARE CORRECTIVE UNDER-GARMENTS...
...BUT WITH THE MONEY I'M SAVING THIS WAY, I CAN BUY TWO OR THREE THIN BOOKS THERE...
BREAST-SMOOSHING UNDERGARMENT
THIN BOOKS = DOUJINSHI
I'M USING THINGS THAT I ALREADY HAVE ON HAND...
GOSO (RUMMAGE)
...SUCH AS...
GOSO
PACKING TAPE
A PLAYER ONCE TOLD ME...
CORRECTIVE?
PACKING TAPE BINDING.
ONCE YOU GET USED TO IT, YOU'LL BE ABLE TO SQUISH 'EM OUT OF SIGHT.
PLAYER = COSPLAYER
BI (RIP)
GURU (SPIN)
THIS IS JUST PRACTICE!
BI
BI
BI

ZURI (SLIP)
URK.
BORON (BOING)
HMM...
THE FIRST PART OF WRAPPING IS THE HARDEST...
BI (RIP)
BI
BI
GURU (SPIN)
GUCHA (SCRUNCH)
GUCHA
YIKES.
RRR...

HFF!
HFF!
THIS IS... KILLING ME...
AND IT'S HOT...
じと…
JITO (EXHAUSTED)
うる
URU (TRICKLE)

BARI (RIP)
LIKE I COULD EVER...
BARI
BARI
...DO THIS AT THE VENUE!
NOW I HAVE EVEN MORE RESPECT FOR PLAYERS!!

BUTT SLIM
A simple way to fix your fanny! Perfect for dressing as a man!
Product name: Butt Slim
Price: 3,480 yen
Amount: 1
Free shipping! Fast delivery!
↓ ↓ ↓
Add to cart
IT'LL LOOK WEIRD IF I DON'T HAVE A SMALLER BUTT...
• BREAST CORRECTER
• BUTT SLIM
TOTAL: 5,430 YEN
POCHI (TIK)
POCHI

Do You Like the Nerdy Nurse?

Do You Like the Nerdy Nurse?

Chapter 17:

Cosplay Is More Than Just Wearing a Costume (Part Two)

I DID WHAT I COULD...
COSTUME CREATION
WIG STYLING
MAKEUP PRAC-TICE
WHILE PREPARING, I WAS PSYCHED...
...BUT NOW THAT IT'S REALLY HERE, I'M NERVOUS!
WILL I BE ABLE TO PUT THE COSTUME ON EFFICIENTLY IN THE CHANGING ROOM?
WILL I LOOK WEIRD?
WILL I MESS UP THE MAKE-UP?
WHAT IF I GET SICK?
AND I'M KIND OF EMBARRASSED ABOUT POSING FOR PHOTOS...
KIME
KIME (POSE)
JUST PRETEND YOU'RE AT A FESTIVAL...
...AND ENJOY DRESSING UP LIKE IZOU-CHAN!
AND I NEED YOU FOR PROMO-TION!
Y...
YOU'RE RIGHT!
GO (RUMBLE)
OH, SORR—

THE FELLOW-FAN HATER!?!?
WHAT ARE THE ODDS!?
GO (RUMBLE)
GO
GO
GO
GO
......
TO (CLACK)
TO
TO
HMPH!
HMPH!
WHAT'LL I DO...
...IF SHE SEES ME IN COSPLAYING FORM?
DON'T WORRY, IT'S A HUGE VENUE!

どやどや
DOYA (CROWDED)
DOYA
AH... CAN I SHAKE YOUR HAND?
EVERY-ONE'S SO FRIENDLY!!
S...
SURE...
YEEE!

I WAS EXTREMELY NERVOUS, BUT...
I NEVER KNEW THERE WAS A WORLD IN WHICH PEOPLE WOULD WANT TO SHAKE MY HAND WHEN I'M DRESSED LIKE THIS.
HOWA (FLUSTERED)
ほわ
CAN I SHAKE YOUR HAND TOO?
ME TOO!
WAWAWA
わわわ
YOU'RE A HIT.
EX-CUSE ME.
ARE YOU GOING TO BE IN THE PHOTOGRAPHY SPACE?
HUH?
WHAT AM I SUP-POSED TO DO ...
...IN THAT PHOTOG-RAPHY SPACE?
HAVING EXPERI-ENCES IS IMPORTANT. JUST GO.
......
SIGN: COSPLAY AREA
コスプレエリア
WAYA (BUZZ)
わや
WAYA
わや
WAYA
わや

THEY'RE ALL SO INTO IT...
KOSO
KOSO (SNEAK)
KASHA
KASHA
KASHA (SNAP)
H-HEY!
IZOU-CHAN-SAN!
BIKU (TWITCH)
CAN I TAKE YOUR PICTURE!?
WHAAA !?
M-ME?
KOKU (NOD)
KOKU
ATA (PANIC)
KYORO
KYORO (GLANCE)
FUTA (FRANTIC)
O... OKAY ...
BUT JUST ONE...

CHI (GLANCE)
チ
CHIRA
チラッ
PASHA
パシャ
CUUUUUUTE!!
TERE
てれ
PASHASHASHA (CLICKETY)
パシャシャシャ
TERE (BASHFUL)
てれ
SHA
シャ
PASHA
パシャ
THAT UNPOLISHED STYLE...
...IS SO IZOU-CHAN.
TH-THANKS...?
THANK YOU!
SORRY I DON'T HAVE MY BUSINESS CARD ON ME...
I...
I WASN'T ABLE TO DO ANYTHING...
I JUST STOOD THERE.
YURA
YURA
あら
ぎょっ
GYO (GOGGLE)
EXCUSE ME, CAN I TAKE A PHOTO TOO?
ME TOO!
あら
YURA (WOBBLE)

カシャ
KASHA (CLICK)
WAIT...
カシャ
KASHA
...A SEC...
カシャ
KASHA
カシャ
KASHA
SQUEEE!
THE FIVE-STAR IZOU-CHAN POSE!
HERE
PHOTOG-RAPHER
I DIDN'T MEAN TO!!

HEY!
EEK!
?
NYŪ (FWOO)
ニュッ
NU (GULP)
ヌッ
CORNERED.
WHAT'S SHE DOING HERE?
PURU
プル
PURU (QUIVER)
プル

I LOVE IT...

IZOU-CHAN...
...IS HERE.
MY IDEAL...
NIKO (GRIN)
DEFENSIVE INSTINCT SMILE
BO (BLUSH)
◎ ※ △ ■ !!!
DA (DASH)
PLEASE DON'T RUN IN THE EXHIBITION AREA!!
...SHE DIDN'T KNOW IT WAS ME?
KAKUN (SLUMP)
THE FOUR-STAR IZOU-CHAN POSE!!
KASHA (SNAP)
KASHA
KASHA
FOUR-STAR!!
IZOU OKADA

JOB WELL DONE.
BUT WASN'T IT FUN?
AND SO INTENSE THAT IT BURNED CALORIES.
GORO
GORO (RUMBLE)
DO (BUMP)
OH, SORR—
GO GO GO GO GO
GO (RUMBLE) GO GO
@t_momomomo_t 1 hour ago
Executed
I challenged myself.
IS THIS MOMO-YAMA-SENSEI ...!?
CAN I ASK HER ABOUT THIS NEXT TIME?
I'M NOT SURE.

Do You Like the Nerdy Nurse?

Do You Like the Nerdy Nurse?

Summer Morning, Part 1
TIRORIRO (JINGLE)
ティロリロ♪
TIRORIRO
ティロリロ♪
TIRORIRO
ティロリロ♪
TIRORIRO
ティロリロ♪
TIRORIRO
ティローリロ♪
MOZO (RUSTLE)
もぞ…
Chapter 18:
A Summer Day with Momoyama-sensei
GACHA (CLATTER)
ガチャ
SHURU (FWISH)
シュル

Summer Morning, Part 1: The End

Summer Morning, Part 2: The End

Summer Afternoon, Part 1

Summer Afternoon, Part 1: The End

Summer Afternoon, Part 2: The End

THE SAME DIRECTION AGAIN...
DOOON (BOOM)
?
WHEN I HAVE MY FIGURES LINED UP...
...JUST LIKE THIS ART...
...THEY'RE ALL GAZING IN THE SAME DIRECTION.
OH, UM...

IT MADE ME WONDER...
...WHAT THE FIGURES ARE LOOKING AT...
GUTA (SLUMP)
SENSEI!?
THEN MAYBE THE FIGURES ARE!...
THEIR POINT OF VIEW...

Summer Afternoon, Part 3: The End

THE NURSE'S OFFICE...
...HAS BECOME A LIVELY PLACE LATELY.
GUGU (STRETCH)
グググッ
STAY HEALTHY, BOYS.
SIGH...
天誅
てんちゅう
SHIRT: DIVINE PUNISHMENT

Summer Night: The End

Do You Like the Nerdy Nurse?

Do You Like the Nerdy Nurse?

MIIN (KRIK)
ONE SUMMER DAY, A BOY IS LOST IN THOUGHT.
MIN
MIIN
BOOO (DAZED)
I WANNA DO SOMETHING ...!!
(NAGUE)
Chapter 19:
Why Don't You Try Writing Something?
IT WAS FUN MAKING THE HEALTH GAZETTE.
GIKO (CREAK)
I ENVY YUZUKI-KUN.
HE'S GOT SO MANY TALENTS.
INCLUDING THE ABILITY TO DRAW...!
THE SPIRIT OF THE BOOKS WHIMSICALLY ASKED HIM...
LIGHT NOVELS
GO (RUMBLE)
GO
...“WHY DON'T YOU TRY WRITING SOMETHING?”
GO
GO
GO
GO

MIIIN (CHIRP)
MIII
MIN
MAYBE GOING TO THE LIBRARY WILL GIVE ME SOME INSPIRATION.
KAA (CAW)
KAA
I'VE NEVER TALKED TO ANYONE ABOUT THIS BEFORE, BUT...
KAA
KAA
CROWS ARE SO COOL.
IN FACT...
...THE TENGU ARE REALLY COOL.
I DON'T KNOW MUCH ABOUT THEM, BUT IN MY IMAGINATION, THEY HAVE A BIRD-LIKE APPEARANCE.
ALL RIGHT, I'LL HAVE A TENGU APPEAR IN MY STORY.
WHAT'S THE CONNECTION...
...BETWEEN DRESSING LIKE A BUDDHIST MONK AND MYSTICAL MOUNTAIN BUDDHISM?
WHEEL OF LIFE!?
THEY FELL OFF IT AND INTO THE TENGU REALM...
WHAT IS THAT? COOL.
HUH? THIS IS FASCINATING...
BOOK: SUPERNATURAL MONSTERS GUIDEBOOK

IKI (FLASH)
IKI
TO BE HONEST, I DIDN'T UNDERSTAND MUCH OF THAT...
...BUT I HAVE A FEELING IT REALLY OPENS UP MY STORY!
WAKU (EXCITED)
MY MIND'S ON FIRE!
WAKU
A TENGU WITH SUPER-NATURAL POWERS...
HE'S A TEACHER...
REMOVED FROM THE WHEEL OF LIFE
TENGU
GODS
TITANS
HUMAN
HUNGRY GHOSTS
ANIMAL
HELL
SAD PAST
ENEMY FORCES
MIIIN
MIN
MIN
BUT I CAN'T THINK OF A STORY TO PUT IT ALL TOGETHER...
HOT...
MIIIN
MIN
BO (CRACK)
ONE MORE!

AH...
YUZUKI-KUN.
DOSA (FWUMP)
ZA (SHK)
BO (CRACK)
TO
HE'S DOING BASE-BALL PRACTICE IN THIS HEAT.
WOW.
SAWA (RUSTLE)
TO
KUA (YAWN)
SAWA
BO
ZA

HYUN (WHIZZZ)
ヒュー
HA (GASP)
SOMETHING...
SU (SHFF)
...CAME OUT OF THE SKY!!
ZUSHI (LURCH)
!?
MY BODY FEELS HEAVY...
DO (THUD)
?
?
KURA (WOBBLE)
HUH...?
DOSA (WHUMP)

WHITE LIGHT.
CHILLY AIR.
I DOZED OFF.
A HAND...?

GOOD MORNING.
HOW DO YOU FEEL?

GABA (RISE)
がばっ
MOMO-YAMA-SENSEI'S HAND...!
IT WAS SOFT AND SLIGHTLY COOL...
A WOMAN'S HAND...
WHO WROTE ABOUT BEING CAREFUL OF HEATSTROKE IN THE LATEST ISSUE OF THE HEALTH GAZETTE?
BE AWARE OF YOUR BODY'S CONDITION.
...I DID.
※PLEASE BE CAREFUL ABOUT HEAT-STROKE!!
YEAH, THAT'S IT! I'LL MAKE THE TENGU A COOL WOMAN.
THE MAIN CHARACTER WILL BE A BOY WHO GETS LOST IN THE MOUNTAINS, WHERE THERE'S A TENGU...
WAKU (EXCITED)
わく
WAKU
わく

YOU LOOK LIKE...
...YOU'RE HAVING A GOOD TIME.
HUH?
ドキッ
DOKI (BADUM)
シャッ
SHA (SHF)
FROM HER OWN EXPERIENCE, MOMOYAMA-SENSEI CAN TELL WHEN SOMEONE IS FANTASIZING.
I GOT A LOT OF IDEAS TODAY!
NEW NOTEBOOK
Notebook
NOW'S THE TIME TO START WRITING!

WHAT SHOULD THE TITLE BE?
FLASHING WINGS
THE WHEEL OF LIFE
FLASHING RAVEN HAIR
A FLASH OF RAVEN HAIR
WAKU (EXCITED)
わく
WAKU
わく
AND NOW TO START WRITING!
NO.
DATE
FLASHING WINGS
THE WHEEL OF LIFE
FLASHING RAVEN HAIR
A FLASH OF RAVEN HAIR
KOCHI (TICK)
コチ
KOCHI
コチ
KOCHI
コチ
KOCHI
コチ
......
I'M GONNA PLAY FGO.
GOROOON (LOUNGE)

Do You Like
the Nerdy
Nurse?

Do You Like the Nerdy Nurse?

ISHIN☆LIVE
AUGUST EVENT SCENARIO
Izou Okada
"You feel down because the weather is lousy...?
It's the weather's fault?"
Chapter 20:
Drawing Is Fun
MMMM...!!
Izou Okada
"How about if I hold this and sing you a song?"
SHIRT: MIC ALL THE WAY

FOR ABOUT TWO DAYS...
...NIJIKO MOMOYAMA HAD BUTTERFLIES IN HER STOMACH.
NO GOOD...
TUNKU
TUNKU (THUNK)
I CAN'T STOP THE THROBBING IN MY CHEST!!
IZOU-CHAN... WHAT A GUY...
HE'S THE EMBODIMENT OF "PITIFUL = CUTE"...
AND THAT AURA...
THANK YOU! THANK YOU FOR THE EVENT SCENARIO!
SHIRT: MIC ALL THE WAY
EVEN IF I SHOUT ABOUT IT ON SOCIAL MEDIA, IT'S STILL LIKE AN ECHO CHAMBER IN MY HEAD.
AT THIS RATE, I CAN'T EVEN FOCUS ON MY WORK!
MY HEAD HURTS...
WHAT SHOULD I DO AT A TIME LIKE THIS...?

...!
PRODUCING SOMETHING...
DRAW...
DRAW...!?
ME!?

OH, BUT...
I'M NOT GOOD AT IT, THOUGH...
...UP THROUGH HIGH SCHOOL, MY FRIENDS AND I...
WAI (GIGGLE)
ワイ
WAI
ワイ
...HAD FUN WITH OUR SCRIBBLINGS AND SKETCHES.
KYA (SQUEE)
キャッ
KYA
キャッ
BUT WHEN I WENT TO COLLEGE, NO ONE AROUND ME DREW.
WHEN DID I STOP DRAWING...?
ULP!
JUST SAYING "DRAWING" HAS GOT ME GOING!
I KNOW WHAT I NEED!
GASA (RUMMAGE)
ガサ
GOSO (DIG)
ゴソ

DON (DUN-DUN)
TH-THIS BRINGS BACK MEMORIES...
KACHI (CHIK)
DOES THE MARKER STILL WORK...?
AH...
THE SMELL OF AN ALCOHOL-BASED MARKER...
※BE CAREFUL NOT TO SMELL IT TOO MUCH.
I WANT TO DRAW...
...IZOU-CHAN!
I WANT TO GET HIM ON PAPER!
EVEN IF IT'S A CRAPPY DRAWING!
IT DOESN'T MATTER IF I'M COMPETENT OR NOT!

A RECORD OF MY DEEP EMOTIONS AFTER MEETING IZOU-CHAN!
HIS AURA, WHICH EXPANDS IN MY MEMORIES!
I JUST WANT TO RECORD IT!!
I JUST WANT TO DRAW!!!

PITA (FREEZE)
ぴたっ
ULP.
HOW DO YOU DRAW AGAIN?
...AT LEAST HIS FACE!
I LOVE HIS DAZZLING SMILE AND THAT BASHFUL FACE.
I LOVE WHEN HIS HAIR DROOPS DOWN, BUT YOU CAN STILL SEE HIS EYE THROUGH IT.
HUH?
I FEEL KIND OF LIGHT-HEADED...
KORI (SKRITCH)
コリ
KORI
コリ
STRANGE... I HAD A HEADACHE BEFORE...
...AND THIS POSTURE ISN'T PARTICULARLY COMFORTABLE.
GUGU (CREAK)
ぐぐっ
IT'S LIKE I DON'T FEEL THE WEIGHT OF MY OWN BODY!
MY HABITUAL NEGATIVITY IS GONE!
IS THIS EUPHORIA!?
DOPAMINE!?
SA (SQUEAK)
サッ
SA
サッ

I LOVE DRAWING !!
THIS IS FUN...!!!
KOTO (CLUNK)
コト
I DREW HIM! ♡ I DREW HIM! ♡
WHETHER IT'S GOOD OR NOT, I'M CONTENT! ♡
BUT WHAT SHOULD I DO WITH IT...?
DRAWING IS FINE, BUT...
...

KASHA (CLICK)
カシャ
THERE.
IF I PUT IT ON SOCIAL MEDIA, KURITA-KUN WILL SEE IT...
I GUESS THAT'S OKAY.
I DON'T MIND IF KURITA-KUN SEES IT.
('ω')ノ @eiatwp ...5 minutes ago
返信先:@_t_momomomo_tさん
Your boyfriend!? Did you draw your boyfriend!? Hah? Cute!
@t_mom
返信先:@eiatwpさん
That's right.
NERD FRIEND
Executed
HEE HEE.
HEE HEE HEE.

Do You Like the Nerdy Nurse?

Do You Like
the Nerdy
Nurse?

THIS SUMMER'S SECOND EVENT AT THE UPSIDE-DOWN PYRAMID.
Chapter 21:
Will I Be Able to Express How I Feel!?
THIS EVENT TAKES PLACE FOUR TIMES A YEAR.
GOOD MORNING.
GOOD MORNING.
CREATIVE WORKS ARE LINED UP SHOULDER TO SHOULDER, FROM PROS AND AMATEURS ALIKE.
THE ATMOSPHERE IS MUCH MORE SUBDUED THAN DURING THE COSPLAY EVENT THE VENUE HOSTED ONLY DAYS AGO.
NIJIKO MOMOYAMA'S FIGHTING SPIRIT...
...BURNS QUIETLY.
GUIDE

10:30 A.M.
GUIDE

9:15 A.M.
YOU KNOW WHAT YOU WANNA BUY, MOMO?
YES...
AT THE WALL CIRCLE...
"WALL CIRCLE"...
...REFERS TO POPULAR CIRCLES THAT ARE SEATED WITH THEIR BACKS NEAR A WALL TO PROVIDE SPACE FOR THEIR WARES AND FOR CUSTOMERS TO LINE UP.
("CIRCLE" HERE MEANS A GROUP—OR INDIVIDUALS WITHIN A GROUP—THAT CREATES THEIR OWN MANGA.)
壁サークル
島中
TABLES: WALL CIRCLE / ISLAND
THE MANGA SHE PUT ONLINE WAS SOOOO GOOD.
THEN SHE SUDDENLY STARTED SELLING BOOKS, SO EVERYONE WAS DYING TO GET IN ON THE GROUND FLOOR.
I'M EXPECTING A LONG LINE...
...BUT IF POSSIBLE, I WANT TO CONVEY MY GRATITUDE TO THE CREATOR AND HOW MOVED I WAS WHEN I FIRST READ HER MANGA...

SO THANK YOU FOR GETTING ME INTO THIS EVENT EARLY!
09:00
10:00
11:00
Circles open for business
Doors open
SINCE YOU'RE HELPING ME SET UP, SELL, AND ARE A CUSTOMER YOURSELF, NO PROBLEM!
CIRCLE LEADER
9:30 A.M.
NO ONE'S LINING UP FOR THE WALL CIRCLE.
LOOKS LIKE THE MEMBERS OF THE CIRCLE AREN'T HERE YET EITHER...
HEH-HEH, I BOUGHT THE CATALOG.
THIS ONE HAS AN INTERVIEW WITH ONE OF MY FAVORITE NEW AUTHORS.
I'LL READ IT WHILE I'M STANDING IN LINE.
ALL ABOUT THE EVENT
FRONT VIEW
MAGAZINE: TEARS MAGAZINE
10:00 A.M.
IS THIS OKAY FOR THE POSTER?
IT'S PERFECT! THANKS!
THE CROWD AROUND THE WALL CIRCLE IS GETTING BIGGER...
IS IT ALL RIGHT IF I GET IN LINE OVER THERE?
SURE, WHY NOT?

I SHALL RETURN...!
BISHI (FWIP)
ビシッ
GOOD LUCK!
AND THEN DO THAT ERRAND FOR ME!
IT LOOKS LIKE SHE'S GIVING HER BOOK TO CIRCLE ACQUAINTANCES FIRST.
COULD YOU WAIT FOR THE OFFICIAL TIME...?
THEN...
...DOES THAT MEAN...?
OZU (HESITANT)
おず…

I'M AT THE HEAD OF THE LINE...!!
HOW MANY TIMES IN MY LIFE HAVE I EVER BEEN FIRST IN LINE...?
I-IT SEEMS LIKE THE ONE WITH HER HAIR DOWN IS THE AUTHOR...
THERE... SHE'S STANDING RIGHT THERE...
SOWA (FIDGET)
SOWA
SOWA
WHOA...
SHE'S GORGEOUS...
SOWA
SOWA
SOWA
LEADER OF THE CIRCLE
SOWA
SOWA
SOWA
SOWA
WILL I BE ABLE TO EXPRESS HOW I FEEL!?
I LOVE EACH AND EVERY ONE OF YOUR CHARACTERS.
IT HITS ME RIGHT IN THE CHEST!
IT'S OVER-FLOWING WITH EMOTIONS.
I LOVE YOUR DRAWINGS!
YOU HAVE SO MUCH ARTISTIC SENSE!
IT'S WONDERFUL!
I LOVE IT!
GURU (SPIN)
GURU
AT THE VERY LEAST, I DON'T WANT TO SAY ANYTHING RUDE OR BE A PAIN...!
MAYBE I'M ALREADY BEING A NUISANCE BY STANDING HERE SO LONG!?
10:30 A.M.
STAFF MEMBERS ARE MILLING AROUND NOW...
IS EVERYONE HERE TO SEE "KAERU-DOU"-SAN?
Y-YES.

ZURAAA (CROWD)
ズラ
CHIRA (GLANCE)
チラ
I'M GOING TO LEAD THE LINE OUTSIDE OF THE VENUE, SO PLEASE FOLLOW ME.
WOW...!
MY FIRST EXPERIENCE! PART OF A LONG LINE MOVING INTO STANDBY POSITION TO SEE A WALL CIRCLE...
ZORO (SHUFFLE)
ぞろ
...AND I'M AT THE HEAD OF IIIT!!
ZORO
ぞろ
ZORO
ぞろ

10:58 A.M.
TWO MINUTES UNTIL IT STARTS.
(THE DESK ARRANGEMENT CHANGED TOO.)
SA (SWF)
I'M GOING TO BUY THE NEW VOLUME AND THE OLD ONE AGAIN!
DOKI (THUMP)
DOKI
HAVE TO BE CAREFUL I DON'T DROP MY MONEY OR MY THINGS...!
TONS OF PEOPLE BEHIND ME, SO I CAN'T AFFORD TO DAWDLE!
PRESSURE
AND ALSO!!
DOKI
I HAVE TO TELL THE AUTHOR HOW I FEEL ABOUT HER BOOK...!!
DOKI
11:00 A.M.

PACHI (CLAP)
パチ
PACHI
パチ
PACHI
パチ
PACHI
パチ
Comitia is now open!
THE CLAPPING IS A MARK OF THE MORE RE-STRAINED COMITIA.
ZUA (CLEAN)
ズアッ
I'LL TAKE ONE COPY EACH OF THE NEW BOOK AND THE PREVIOUS ONE, PLEASE!
THANK YOU!
I GOT IT...!
圧ッ
PRESSURE
!!!
AH!
THAT'S RIGHT! I HAVE TO TELL HER HOW I FEEL!
BA (TURN)
バッ
YIKES!

YOUR COMIC IS WONDERFUL!
I LOVE IT!
I'M ROOTING FOR YOU !!

PA (FLASH)
ぱっ
THANK YOU!!
I...
I SAID IIIIIT!!
I GOT IT! I TOLD HER!
ALL RIGHT !!
I WAS ABLE TO TELL HER DIRECTLY THAT I LOVED IT.
I'M SO HAPPY RIGHT NOW.
AFTER THAT, THE EXCITEMENT AND CONFIDENCE CONTINUED TO INCREASE IN HER THROUGHOUT THE DAY...
WHAT A GREAT TIME...
...UNTIL GETTING HOME, AT WHICH TIME SHE PROMPTLY COLLAPSED.

COME TO THINK OF IT, I NEVER BOUGHT THE FINAL VOLUME.
EVEN THOUGH I LOVED THE SERIES AND BOUGHT EACH NEW VOLUME AS SOON AS IT CAME OUT...
PERA (FLIP)
ペラ
HOW COULD I HAVE SUDDENLY JUST LOST INTEREST?
MAYBE...
...I DIDN'T LOVE IT AS MUCH AS I THOUGHT.
NO, THAT'S NOT IT...
I JUST LOVED SOMETHING ELSE TOO AND WANTED TO PURSUE THAT...
...I LOVE IT.
YOU'RE IN LOVE WITH...
...MOMO-CHAN-SENSEI, AREN'T YOU?

DOKIN (BADUM)
ドキン
URGH ...
WHY MOMOYAMA-SENSEI...?
FURU
ふる
FURU (SHAKE)
ふる
WHAT DOES...
..."LOVE" MEAN ...?
KOTO (CLUNK)
コト

Do You Like
the Nerdy
Nurse?

SEPTEMBER
KAA (CAW)
KAA
GUESS I'LL CALL IT A DAY.
PATAN (SHUT)
WELL, IT'S THE START OF A NEW SEMESTER.
WE SHOULD BOTH BE GETTING HOME.
...
Final Chapter: There Are All Kinds of Love
HUH? IT'S THAT LATE ALREADY?
I HAVE TO LOCK UP HERE...
TH-THEN...
...I'LL WALK WITH YOU!

SO WE LIVE IN THE SAME DIRECTION.
YEAH.
KASU
カス
SOUNDS LIKE YOU HAVE A SORE THROAT?
JUST MY VOICE. I THOUGHT IT WAS A COLD... BUT I'VE HAD IT FOR DAYS NOW.
KASU
カス
KASU (RASP)
カス
THAT BUILDING...
KASU
カス
OH!
THEN YOUR VOICE...
...MIGHT BE BREAKING!
THIS SOON?
SOME PEOPLE SUDDENLY REALIZE THAT THEIR VOICE HAS BECOME LOWER.
IT'S DIFFERENT FOR EVERYONE.
THE TIME WHEN A BOY'S VOICE CHANGES DIFFERS FROM PERSON TO PERSON TOO.
BUT IT'S AN AMAZING THING!
I'M MOVED!
KURU (FWISH)
くるっ

THE MOMENT A PERSON MATURES...
...AND IT'S RIGHT BEFORE MY VERY EYES!
GROWING AND MATURING IS INCREDIBLE.
WHENEVER I READ BOYS' MANGA, I BOTH TEAR UP AND GET FIRED UP.
HAVE YOU SEEN THE POSTER FOR YOWAMUSHI PEDAL, WITH THE SOHOKU HIGH CAPTAIN...?

UM...
THIS IS FROM OUT OF THE BLUE...
...BUT HAS IT EVER...
...CROSSED YOUR MIND...
...THAT YOU MIGHT NOT LOVE SOMETHING...
...AS MUCH AS YOU ONCE THOUGHT?
HUH? HMMM...
WHEN I TALKED TO SOMEONE WHO LOVES THE SAME THING I DO...
A CERTAIN FELLOW-FAN HATER
...I WAS AFRAID THAT MAYBE...
...HER "LOVE" WAS SUPERIOR TO MINE, BUT...
ANYWAY, WHAT ABOUT IT?
YOU DIDN'T READ THE FINAL VOLUME!?
ME TOO! I LOVED THE MANGA SERIES...
...BUT THE LAST VOLUME...
I HATE TO ADMIT IT...
...I JUST READ THE SPOILERS ONLINE!

OH, LO AND BEHOLD!
A BOOK-STORE!!!
DOOON (BAM)
I-IF I HAVE POCKET CHANGE ON ME...
COME ON IN!
SIGN: BOOKS
THANK GOOD-NESS!!
CONGRATU-LATIONS!!
PACHI (CLAP)
PACHI
URGH...
THE FINAL VOLUME...

WHAT IF YOU LOVED IT SO MUCH...
...YOU DIDN'T WANT IT TO END...?
...COULD THAT BE WHY?
YEAH.
TOMORROW...
BUT NOW...
...WE'LL BE ABLE TO CHAT ALL ABOUT IT!
......
AND THE DAY AFTER TOMORROW AND SO ON...

I WANT TO...
...TALK TO YOU EVERY DAY, SENSEI.
SURE, JUST COME TO THE NURSE'S OFFICE.
TH-THAT'S NOT WHAT I MEAN!
I'M NOT SURE...
...BUT MAYBE...
...THE "LOVE" I FEEL...
...IS DIFFERENT FROM...
..."LOVING" TO TALK ABOUT...
...MANGA AND GAMES.

KURITA-KUN...
THERE ARE...
...ALL KINDS OF "LOVE."

"DREAMS" AND "PAIRINGS"...
...FOR EXAMPLE.
TAKE A CERTAIN ROMANTIC SIM FOR WOMEN...
A DATING SIM...
THE MAIN GOAL IS FOR THE PLAYER TO HAVE A ROMANTIC RELATIONSHIP WITH ONE OF THE CHARACTERS IN THE GAME.
SCREEN: HANDSOME GUYS PUZZLE
I WENT WITH MY FIRST IMPRESSION AND DECIDED TO GO FOR A CERTAIN CHARACTER...
I LOVE YA, BABY.
UGH, NO THANKS.
WHEN HE STARTED FAWNING ON ME...
...I REALIZED HE WASN'T THE ONE.
AFTER ONE THING AND ANOTHER...
...I FOUND MY FAVORITE.
I LOVE YOU.
AH!

WE LOVED EACH OTHER...
...BUT SOMETHING SEEMED OFF.
TO THE PLAYER, WITH THE PLEASANT CHARACTER...
...THERE WAS "LOVE."
= DREAM
OH!
HE'S LOVE-STRUCK!
HAAA (SIGH)
BE HAPPY TOGETHER!
AND FOR THE MAIN CHARACTER, THE CHARACTER SHE GETS INVOLVED WITH...
...THERE'S MAYBE A DIFFERENT "LOVE."
= PAIRING
MAY-BE...
...THAT'S SIMILAR?
I HAVE A FEELING IT'S NOT...
...BUT THERE ARE MANY DIFFERENT KINDS OF LOVE FOR YOU TOO, HUH, SENSEI?

MOMO-YAMA-SENSEI...
...CAN I ASK YOU...
...WHAT YOUR "FAVOR-ITE"...
...IN THAT GAME IS LIKE?
WELL, LET'S SEE...
I WANTED TO SEE MY "FAVORITE" SO BADLY...
...THAT WHENEVER I TURNED THE GAME ON...

...I FELT LIKE I WAS WALKING ON AIR.
MAYBE IT WAS CLOSE TO WHAT REAL LOVE FEELS LIKE.

HEY, SENSEI.
I'M CURIOUS ABOUT THAT DATING SIM.
WHAAA!?
NO, LISTEN, THE AUDIENCE IS WORKING WOMEN...
OH, BUT THE ANIME VERSION STARTS IN OCTOBER!
THAT REMINDS ME. I WANT TO GO OVER THE FALL ANIME SHOWS WITH YOU.
I JUST HOPE I HAVE ROOM ON MY HARD DRIVE.
Do You Like the Nerdy Nurse?: The End

Do You Like the Nerdy Nurse?

BONUS
MOMO...
...YOU WOULDN'T DO THIS KIND OF COSPLAY?
DEFINITELY NOT.
WHO AM I COSPLAYING HERE?

EVERY-ONE IS EXPECTING THAT...
...AND I'D LIKE TO SEE IT TOO.
SOMETHING THAT A MAN OR WOMAN COULD PULL OFF WOULD BE GOOD.
SOMETHING LIKE THIS
FORGET IT.
IF I DID IT AGAIN, I'D LIKE TO GO AS TAKECHI-SAN...
...AND ROAM AROUND THE EXPO WITH IZOU-CHAN.
DOUJINSHI
YOU'RE TEMPTING ME!!
YOU'RE TALL, SO HEIGHT-WISE, WE WOULD BE THE PERFECT PAIR!
MEAN-WHILE, IN CLASS...
I ADMIRE COSPLAYERS.
IT'S KIND OF TOUGH FOR ME.
HUH?
MY BIG SISTER LIKES TO DRESS ME UP.
YUZUKI-KUN, YOUR SISTER REALLY LOVES YOU, HUH...?
SHE JUST USES ME.
BUT I'M IMPRESSED THAT YOU GO ALONG WITH IT.

THE END

AFTERWORD

THANK YOU FOR READING *DO YOU LIKE THE NERDY NURSE?* I'M ARATA KAWABATA.

THIS TWO-VOLUME SERIES WAS PUBLISHED ON THE WEBSITE YAWARAKA SPIRITS OVER THE SPACE OF A YEAR EXACTLY. IN THE BEGINNING, WHEN IT WAS JUST GOING TO BE A ONE-SHOT STORY, MY EDITOR SAID, "WHY DON'T YOU DO IT LIKE THIS?" I THOUGHT OF MYSELF AS SOMEONE WHO LIKES TO DRAW, AND THAT'S WHAT I HAD DONE, ESPECIALLY WITH MY PREVIOUS WORK, *SHINGUN NO CADET*, SO I WAS LIKE, "WHY???" (LOL). THE QUESTION OF DRAWING A MALE OR FEMALE ASIDE, I LOVED THE THOUGHT OF DOING A NERD STORY. I LOVE IT, BUT IT WAS TOO MUNDANE FOR ME, SINCE IT'S MY NORMAL LIFE, SO AT EVERY STORY CONFERENCE WITH MY EDITOR, WE WOULD CHITCHAT ABOUT NERDY STUFF. THEY WOULD PINPOINT THE MOST INTERESTING STUFF AND WE WOULD CRAFT A CHAPTER AROUND THAT. THAT'S HOW WE DID IT EVERY TIME.

FOR THE TOPICS AND DETAILS, I HAVE MY FRIENDS TO THANK. K-NEESAN, WHO LIVES THE OTAKU LIFE, IS INCREDIBLE. K-NEESAN, THIS PAST YEAR, TONS OF ANIME MERCHANDISE FILLED UP MY ROOM, AND IT'S THANKS TO YOU. THOSE LITTLE DOLLS ARE ADORABLE... I TOTALLY GET THE DESIRE TO PARADE THEM AROUND. WHEN I WENT OUT WITH MINE (*DETECTIVE CONAN*'S FURUYA-SAN AND KAZAMI-SAN), I WAS SO AFRAID THEY WOULD GET DIRTY THAT I PUT THEM IN A ZIPLOC BAG. A GOOD MEMORY I HAVE IS OF SOMEONE TELLING ME THEY LOOKED LIKE "SEIZED EVIDENCE." I GOT A LOT MORE FIGURES DURING THAT TIME TOO. WHEN I WANTED A CERTAIN ONE, MY FRIEND (HERE TOO, K-NEESAN) WOULD QUICKLY INVESTIGATE AND PASS ON THE INFO ABOUT WHICH SHOP WAS SELLING IT FOR THE CHEAPEST PRICE.

I WAS MOVED BY THAT, AND THE EXCITEMENT IT ENGENDERED IN ME WAS LIKE A DOOR OPENING TO A NEW WORLD. THAT WAS SO MUCH FUN. RIGHT NOW, THOUGH, I'M TRYING TO PUT THE BRAKES ON MY EVER-EXPANDING FIGURE COLLECTION.

ON THE ONE HAND, I WAS ENJOYING MYSELF, BUT ON THE OTHER, I SOMETIMES WORRIED ABOUT "LAND MINES" IN MY NERD NEIGHBORHOOD(?). BY "LAND MINES," I MEAN PERSONAL ELEMENTS THAT ARE HARD TO SEE, BUT THAT PEOPLE CAN BE EXTREMELY TOUCHY ABOUT, AND COULD DO TERRIBLE EMOTIONAL DAMAGE IF TOUCHED ON. DETERMINING THE LINE BETWEEN WHAT SHOULD BE PERMITTED AND WHAT SHOULDN'T WAS DIFFICULT. I EVEN HAD TROUBLE TELLING MY EDITOR THINGS OCCASIONALLY. I HAVE MEMORIES OF WHEN THE FIRST VOLUME CAME OUT, OF EXPENDING A LOT OF TIME AND EMOTIONS PERSUADING PEOPLE THAT I HAD REMOVED ANY POTENTIAL LAND MINES FROM THE WORK. WHAT REALLY SAVED ME WERE THE WARM RESPONSES I GOT IMMEDIATELY FROM READERS WHEN THE SERIES WAS PUBLISHED ON THE NET.

THIS WORK IS MY JOURNAL AS WELL AS A COMMUNICATION TOOL, BECAUSE THAT'S WHAT MANGA IS FOR ME. THE SERIES ENDS HERE, BUT AFTER READING IT, IF YOU FEEL MOVED ENOUGH TO TALK ABOUT IT, I WOULD LOVE TO HEAR FROM YOU IN ANY FORMAT.

SO THIS IS IT, BUT I PRAY THAT ALL OF YOU TREASURE WHATEVER IT IS THAT YOU LOVE AND THAT IT MAKES YOU HAPPY.

OCTOBER 2019, WRITTEN WHILE AWAITING THE ARRIVAL OF THE POSSIBLY DEVASTATING MAJOR TYPHOON NUMBER NINETEEN, THE NIGHT BEFORE THE NEW RELEASE OF THE TWELVE KINGDOMS.

ARATA KAWABATA

BOUGHT IT TO
ST BOUGHT IT TO TRY
JUST BOUGHT IT TO TRY ON
JUST BOUGHT IT TO TRY ON,
I JUST BOUGHT IT TO TRY ON,
I JUST BOUGHT IT TO TRY ON,
I JUST BOUGHT IT TO TRY ON,
JUST BOUGHT IT TO TRY ON,
JUST BOUGHT IT TO TRY O
UST BOUGHT IT TO TRY ON,
BOUGHT IT TO TRY
OUGHT IT TO

☆ SPECIAL THANKS ☆

MY EDITOR, THE DESIGNER, MY ASSISTANTS, MY FRIENDS, AND THE READERS.

TRANSLATION NOTES

COMMON HONORIFICS
no honorific: Indicates familiarity or closeness; if used without permission or reason, addressing someone in this manner would constitute an insult.
-san: The Japanese equivalent of Mr./Mrs./Miss. If a situation calls for politeness, this is the fail-safe honorific.
-sama: Conveys great respect; may also indicate that the social status of the speaker is lower than that of the addressee.
-shi: An impersonal honorific used in formal speech or writing, e.g. legal documents.
-dono: Roughly equivalent to "master" or "milord."
-kun: Used most often when referring to boys, this indicates affection or familiarity. Occasionally used by older men among their peers, but it may also be used by anyone referring to a person of lower standing.
-chan: An affectionate honorific indicating familiarity used mostly in reference to girls; also used in reference to cute persons or animals of either gender.
-tan: A cutesy version of -chan.
-(o)nii/(o)nee: Meaning "big brother"/ "big sister," it can also refer to those older but relatively close in age to the speaker. It is typically followed by *-san*, *-chan*, or *-sama*.
-senpai: An honorific for one's senior classmate, colleague, etc., although not as senior or respected as a sensei ("teacher").

GENERAL
One hundred yen is roughly equal to one U.S. dollar.

Otaku is a Japanese word referring to obsessive fans. Although it often refers to fans of anime, manga, and video games, the term can apply to any sort of fandom. For example, hard-core baseball fans are called baseball *otaku*.

PAGE 12
Bakumatsu refers to the waning days of the Tokugawa Shogunate and by extension the end of the Edo period in 1868. The term means "end times of the shogunate." All the Bakumatsu Academy characters come from this period.

PAGE 15
Animate is a popular chain with locations all over Tokyo, and the largest retailer of anime, video games, and manga in Japan. As Momoyama explains, it offers a limited-time lottery for certain series, typically costing around six or seven dollars for a single ticket. The odds of getting the rarer items are generally not in the player's favor.

PAGE 17
The art of animation involves the creation of certain frames that define the action, which are known as **key frames** (*genga* in Japanese). These are in contrast to in-between frames (*douga* in Japanese), which fill in the gaps between key frames and smooth out the animation. The drawing of key frames is typically assigned to the more skilled and experienced animators on a project, thus making them more valuable in the eyes of fans.

PAGE 18
"In spring, the dawn..."—along with the rest of the words being read out loud—are from *The Pillow Book* by Sei Shounagon from the year 1002 CE. It's a collection of essays, poems, and other musings by the author about her life as a court lady for an empress consort in the Heian period, and is considered a pioneering work in the informal "rambling" diary style of literature.

PAGE 21
Shipping is a fan term meaning "supporting the idea of certain characters in a romantic relationship." In Japanese, the term originally used is "coupling."

PAGE 27
FGO (or *Fate/Grand Order*) is one of the biggest mobile games in Japan. Based on the Fate franchise, the game's premise is that players are magicians who can summon famous heroes from across time to fight as their servants. In *FGO*, players need to spend in-game currency to summon characters—currency that you can pay for with real money—which means that if you want a rare character, you're at the mercy of random chance. While the Fate franchise began with the 2004 visual novel game *Fate/stay night*, *FGO* is now its most popular incarnation, and regularly tops the mobile game charts in monthly and yearly revenue.

PAGE 28
The character being mentioned here is a psychic-powered antagonist turned antihero from a "certain" magical and scientific light novel series.

PAGE 33
Fujoshi is a humorously self-deprecating term for fans of the Boys Love genre, which focuses on romantic and idealized depictions of male same-sex relationships, and was originally meant for a non-gay female audience. The term is a pun on the word *fujoshi*, meaning "grown woman," but with the *fu* portion replaced by the word for "rotten" (also pronounced *fu*).

PAGE 54
Golden Week is a roughly weeklong holiday period in Japan that begins April 29 and ends in early May.

PAGE 55
Detective Conan, also known as ***Case Closed***, is a popular, long-running manga and anime series that features a high school detective named Shinichi Kudo who is transformed into a child and, in his new identity as Conan Edogawa, solves cases with the help of his childhood friend and love interest, Ran Mori.

A *Detective Conan* **movie** usually comes out during Golden Week with enormous box office success, making the films something of an annual tradition.

PAGE 56
Amupi is a fan nickname for Toru Amuro (alias Rei Furuya), a recurring double agent character in *Detective Conan*. He is notably popular with older female fans.

PAGE 57
The connection between Toru Amuro and **Yuya Kazami** in *Detective Conan* is also part of a running meta-joke involving the long-running Gundam giant robot franchise and its voice actors. Toru Amuro is voiced by Toru Furuya, who is famous for voicing the protagonist of the first *Mobile Suit Gundam* anime, Amuro Ray. Yuya Kazami is voiced by Nobuo Tobita, who played Kamille Bidan, the protagonist of *Mobile Suit Zeta Gundam*—the sequel to the first anime. The *Detective Conan* characters' names are even plays on "Amuro" and "Kamille": Toru Amuro is a combination of Toru (Furuya) and Amuro (Ray), while "Kazami Yuya" resembles the Japanese pronunciation of Kamille (*Kamiiyu*). This history, in turn, lends itself to the shipping of Gundam-inspired characters in *Detective Conan*.

PAGE 60
In *Detective Conan*, Toru Amuro is not only a double agent but also a skilled chef and baker who puts his talents to work as an employee of Café Poirot, occasionally coming up with new recipes for the café.

PAGE 74
"I'll sink myself into this obsession" was originally "I'll sink myself in a swamp" in Japanese, hence the bog. It's a slang term that essentially means "falling into a deep obsession over something."

PAGE 88
Shishinoana is a parody of the Japanese chain store Comic Toranoana originating in Akihabara, which specializes in the selling of amateur fan-made publications known as *doujinshi*. Toranoana means "the tiger's den" (a reference to the similarly named villainous organization from the wrestling manga *Tiger Mask*), whereas Shishinoana means "the lion's den."

PAGES 89-90
Soruto is based on *Boruto*, the follow-up to the popular ninja-themed manga and anime series *Naruto*. This scene resembles how, because *Boruto* stars the children of the characters seen in *Naruto*, many of the characters seen in the first series reappear in the sequel as adults, which leads to fan excitement over which characters ended up in relationships together.

PAGE 98
Gacha refers to games (especially mobile games) that require players to obtain characters through a randomized lottery. The term is derived from the similarly luck-based element of capsule toy dispensers, which are known as *gachapon* (or *gashapon*) in Japan.

PAGE 115
Shinkalion refers to the anime TV series tie-in for Shinkansen Henkei Robo Shinkalion, a Japanese toy franchise featuring bullet trains that can transform into giant robots. In the anime, **Director Hayasugi** is not only the leader of the organization that controls the Shinkalions, but also the father of the main character, Hayato Hayasugi.

PAGE 119
Cavalry battle is an activity for combined athletic events (field days) in Japanese schools, and is especially popular as a trope in manga and anime. Participants form teams with one person as the "rider" and the others acting as their "horses," and the goal is to dislodge the opposing riders or take their headbands.

PAGE 122
98% compatibility is a reference to the anime *Shinkansen Henkei Robo Shinkalion THE ANIMATION*. An AI mascot character named Shashot has the ability to measure a potential pilot's compatibility with the Shinkalion train robots, and 98% would be considered extremely high.

PAGE 130
Blades, like the **Ishi-Blades** depicted in this manga, are a specific type of battery-powered concert glow stick commonly found at idol concerts in Japan. Specific idols within a group often have a thematic color associated with them, so blades are designed to be able to switch colors so fans can show their support for different members at different times.

PAGE 143
Nariakira Shimazu is a historical figure from the *Bakumatsu* period. A feudal lord of the Satsuma Province, his adoption of Western military techniques and technology contributed to the downfall of the Tokugawa Shogunate.

PAGE 161
Ryouma refers to Ryouma Sakamoto, a samurai loyal to the emperor who became an activist against the Tokugawa Shogunate. On the eve of the Meiji Restoration (and the end of the Edo period), he was murdered by pro-Shogunate forces.

PAGE 187
Pitakora is a parody of Havikoro Toy, a chain store in Japan geared toward female *otaku* that buys and sells used goods. **Coaato** is a parody of Lashinbang, a chain that also buys and sells used products but has less of a gender-specific focus. These shops, as well as the rest seen in this chapter, are located in Nakano Broadway, a shopping mall in **Nakano**, Tokyo. There are multiple instances of each store within the mall. As Akihabara has garnered increasing media coverage over the past two decades and more mainstream stores have opened up there, Nakano Broadway has gained a reputation for being where the more serious and hard-core *otaku* go to obtain merchandise.

PAGE 188
Mantenya is a parody of Mandarake, one of the oldest anime and manga goods stores in Japan. Like the other shops, it buys and sells used merchandise. Mandarake's flagship store is in Nakano Broadway, along with its splinter shops found throughout the mall.

PAGE 204
An ***ita*-bag** is a handbag designed to display as much of a person's fan merchandise as possible. Although any bag can potentially be an *ita*-bag, dedicated ones commonly have a clear plastic sleeve around them to prevent buttons and pins from falling off and getting lost. The term literally means "painful bag" and is derived from *itasha*, cars and other vehicles covered from end to end with stereotypically large and garish images of anime characters.

PAGE 206
Fellow fan (*doutan*) and **fellow-fan hater** (*doutan kyohi*) are terms originating from a certain extremely popular but strict Japanese talent agency that specializes in male entertainers.

PAGE 219
Cells at Work! is a manga about the human body, and features personifications of the different cells that keep people alive and running. Characters include white blood cells, red blood cells, platelets, and so on. Numerous spin-offs have also been released, focusing on a variety of topics, from a person in extremely poor health to the various bacteria that also live in the human body.

PAGE 226
A ***doujin* event** is a kind of fair where mostly amateur fans and enthusiasts gather to sell their creations. In addition to *doujinshi* comics, vendors can also be seen selling their own music, prose stories, guidebooks, video games, and more.

An **only *doujin* event** refers to when a *doujin* event is focused on one specific topic or theme, as opposed to allowing a wide variety of subjects.

PAGE 228
High School Entrance Exam Hope is a fictional example of a Japanese cram school, special private schools that provide supplementary classes with the intent of helping students pass Japan's famously rigorous school entrance exams. Cram schools exist for nearly all levels of education, and a student can end up attending different cram schools from elementary school all the way to high school.

PAGE 237
Comiket (short for Comic Market) is Japan's largest and most famous twice-a-year *doujin* event. Beginning in 1975 with only 700 attendees, it has since grown tremendously, with 2019's Winter Comiket seeing an astounding 750,000 attendees over a period of four days.

PAGES 244–247
Mobile games often have different versions of their characters, with rarity being determined by a star rating. A **five-star** character would be harder to obtain than a **four-star** character.

PAGE 254
The **chicken nuggets** are *karaage*, a kind of Japanese fried boneless dark-meat chicken. It's a recurring joke on the Japanese Internet that photos of *karaage* can be digitally edited to look like visually convincing explosions.

PAGE 264
Tengu are a type of mythological creature found in Japanese folklore, and are typically humanoid beings with birdlike features who can use large fans to stir up powerful winds.

PAGE 265
While stories about the origins of *tengu* vary, one idea is that they are Buddhist monks who fell off the Buddhist six-part **Wheel of Life** (*rokudou rinne* in Japanese, *samsara* in Sanskrit) that determines the cycle of reincarnation and into another realm.

PAGE 287
The **upside-down pyramid** refers to Tokyo Big Sight, also known as the Tokyo International Exhibition Center. It is the largest convention center in Japan, and is the site of many exhibitions and events, including Comiket.

Comitia is a *doujin* event held four times a year in Tokyo. Unlike Comic Market and many other events of the kind, Comitia is dedicated solely to original creations not based on any existing works or properties.

PAGE 304
Yowamushi Pedal is a bicycling manga and anime series about a nerdy high school student who's mastered the art of cycling to and from Akihabara, Japan's anime mecca. When his skills are discovered, he's recruited into his school's bicycle racing club, where he competes against talented athletes from all over Japan.

PAGE 321
Katsura is samurai Kogorou Katsura, who helped lead the Meiji Restoration. **Shintarou** is samurai Shintarou Nakaoka, who worked closely with Ryouma Sakamoto in their goal to overthrow Tokugawa.

Do You Like the Nerdy Nurse?

Arata Kawabata

Translation: **SHELDON DRZKA**
Lettering: **PHIL CHRISTIE**

Original Cover Design:
Yoshiyuki SEKI+Keitaro MURATA for VOLARE inc.

Yen Press
150 West 30th Street, 19th Floor,
New York, NY 10001

Visit us at yenpress.com + facebook.com/yenpress + twitter.com/yenpress + yenpress.tumblr.com + instagram.com/yenpress

First Yen Press Edition: February 2021

Yen Press is an imprint of Yen Press, LLC.
The Yen Press name and logo are trademarks of Yen Press, LLC.

Library of Congress Control Number:
2020950210

ISBNs: 978-1-9753-1975-5 (paperback)
978-1-9753-1976-2 (ebook)

10 9 8 7 6 5 4 3 2 1

WOR

Printed in the United States of America